"'To know Christ is to know His benefits'—so said the great reformers of the sixteenth century. Jerry Bridges stands in this same tradition as he brings together the deepest truths of the Christian faith with their practical outcomes in the Christian life. The focus is ever on Jesus Christ, our sole and sufficient Redeemer and Lord. A wonderful primer for every believer!"

—Timothy George, dean, Beeson Divinity School of Samford University; executive editor, *Christianity Today*

"With compelling clarity, Jerry Bridges unwraps the gospel of Jesus Christ in a way that enables us to appropriate and appreciate God's great gift to humanity. In a holistic approach to addressing life's critical questions, Bridges directs us to the Scriptures, focuses us on the Cross, leads us to a relationship with Christ, and unveils for us a way of living that makes a difference. For the inquirer and for the initiated, *The Gospel for Real Life* is a book to be read and read again."

—Stephen B. Kellough, D.Min., Presbyterian minister (PCUSA) and chaplain of Wheaton College (IL)

"Jerry Bridges has written a book with phenomenal clarity and preciseness in helping us understand the gospel of the Lord Jesus. This book is needed by all of us. Jerry has said that we need to preach the gospel to ourselves every day. This book will help us do that with greater understanding and communication. I'm praying that all of our staff and co-laborers will read it."

—Alan Andrews, president, U.S. Navigators

"With his characteristic clarity, compassion, and humility, Jerry Bridges brings the blessings of heaven to the realities of earth—and to the soft places of the heart where those blessings are most needed and most strengthening."

—Dr. Bryan Chapell, president, Covenant Theological Seminary

"In language that is clear and concise, *The Gospel for Real Life* unfolds the whole gospel in a way that not only informs the mind, but also encourages the soul to praise God. The body of Christ is indebted to Jerry Bridges for a much needed presentation of the plan of redemption."

—Robert M. Norris, pastor, Fourth Presbyterian Church, Bethesda, Maryland

"Jerry Bridges has the happy knack of hitting the biblical nail right on the head—in a way that makes it stick. Like John Bunyan before him, he sees us raking about in the dirt when there is a crown of gold above our heads. Our problem as Christians is simply this: we don't believe and understand the gospel very well. It is that simple. It is that radical. Read *The Gospel for Real Life* carefully. It will do you good!"

—Sinclair B. Ferguson, minister of St. George's-Tron Church, Glasgow, Scotland

THE
GOSPEL
FOR REAL LIFE

THE GOSPEL
FOR REAL LIFE

TURN TO THE LIBERATING POWER
OF THE CROSS . . . EVERY DAY

JERRY BRIDGES

NAVPRESS®

Bringing Truth to Life

NavPress
P.O. Box 35001
Colorado Springs, Colorado 80935

The Navigators is an international Christian organization. Our mission is to reach, disciple, and equip people to know Christ and to make Him known through successive generations. We envision multitudes of diverse people in the United States and every other nation who have a passionate love for Christ, live a lifestyle of sharing Christ's love, and multiply spiritual laborers among those without Christ.

NavPress is the publishing ministry of The Navigators. NavPress publications help believers learn biblical truth and apply what they learn to their lives and ministries. Our mission is to stimulate spiritual formation among our readers.

ISBN 1-57683-507-3

Cover design by Ray Moore
Cover photo from Panoramic Images
Creative Team: Don Simpson, Jacqueline Eaton Blakley, Darla Hightower, Pat Miller

Some of the anecdotal illustrations in this book are true to life and are included with the permission of the persons involved. All other illustrations are composites of real situations, and any resemblance to people living or dead is coincidental.

Bridges, Jerry.
    The Gospel for real life with study guide / Jerry Bridges.-- New pbk.
ed.
      p. cm.
Includes bibliographical references.
    ISBN 1-57683-507-3
    1. Christian life. I. Title.
    BV4501.3.B75 2003
    248.4--dc22
                                2003014813

FOR A FREE CATALOG OF
NAVPRESS BOOKS & BIBLE STUDIES,
CALL 1-800-366-7788 (USA)
OR 1-416-499-4615 (CANADA)

Printed in Canada
2 3 4 5 6 7 8 9 10 / 06 05 04 03

To him who loves us and has freed us from our sins by his blood, and has made us to be a kingdom and priests to serve his God and Father—to him be glory and power for ever and ever! Amen.

—REVELATION 1:5-6

To Him who loves me and has freed me
from my sins, this book is reverently,
lovingly, and gratefully dedicated.

CONTENTS

PREFACE

⸺⟨∘⟩⸺

Some years ago I heard someone say that we should "preach the gospel to ourselves every day." Though I had already been doing that to some degree, the statement brought clarity and focus to my own practice, so I began using it in my ministry to others.

So preaching the gospel to yourself every day is what this book is about. It is intended to answer three questions:

- What is the gospel we should preach to ourselves?
- Why do *we, who are already believers,* need to preach it to ourselves?
- How do we do it?

This book is not meant to be a theological treatise. To borrow an expression from the collegiate world, it is intended to be "Gospel 101." This does not mean it is targeted only to new believers. All of us, regardless of how long we have known Christ, need to bathe ourselves in the gospel every day. I pray this book will help us do that.

One of the joys of writing a preface is the opportunity to express appreciation to those who have helped me in my task. Foremost is Mrs. Tracie Bremner, who graciously volunteered to type the manuscript. (Even a computer does not make me a good typist.) Thank you, Tracie. Thanks also to Dr. Dan Doriani, Jim and Beth Luebe, Mark McElmurry, and my pastor, Joseph Wheat, for reading the manuscript and offering helpful comments and suggestions. Thanks to my wife, Jane, for her patient endurance and for reading the manuscript to ensure that it is indeed "Gospel 101" and not a theological treatise. My good friend and editor, Don Simpson, has been a constant help and encouragement. Thank you, Don.

The prayer support of others is a necessity in a project such as this, and I have felt that need more keenly with this book than any other. Although a number of friends have prayed for me, I want to especially thank C. J. Mahaney and the staff at Covenant Life Church for your prayers and continual encouragement. You've waited a long time for this book, and you nudged me along when the going was tough. Thanks also to all the rest of you who prayed. I trust God has answered your prayers.

CHAPTER ONE

UNSEARCHABLE RICHES

M y friend had just learned that the artificial hip he had
received eleven years earlier needed to be replaced. The
previous month, he had had angioplasty to open a clogged
artery to his heart. Along with all this, he suffers from rheuma-
toid arthritis. Signs of old age? Not at all. My friend is only
fifty-six years old.

A few years ago psychiatrist Scott Peck began one of his
books with a three-word sentence: "Life is difficult."[1] He was
right. We live in a sin-cursed world ravaged not only by the
forces of nature and disease, but even more so by people's sinful actions toward one another. No one is exempt. If you're
not experiencing some form of heartache or difficulty at this
time, cheer up—it will surely come sooner or later! Even as
I have been trying to write this chapter, I've been going
through a series of nettlesome and discouraging setbacks.
And I've gotten down on myself because "Christians aren't
supposed to get discouraged."

Sometimes it seems that circumstances are even worse for
Christians. In addition to all the frustrations and heartaches of
life common to everyone, we have an enemy—the Devil—who
"prowls around like a roaring lion looking for someone to
devour" (1 Peter 5:8). Even in our success we feel tension. A

ministry colleague recently confessed that he felt overwhelmed and anxious even in the midst of a fruitful ministry.

Underlying all the other problems we face, however, is the greatest problem of all—our sin. Not the sins of other people against us, as painful as those may be, but our own sin against God. Sin brings with it a sense of guilt, condemnation, and alienation from God. As one dear Christian woman expressed it, "I know God loves me, but sometimes I wonder if He likes me."

What was she saying? How can God love her and not like her? She was saying, "I know God loves me and sent His Son to die for me, but because of my repeated sins and shortcomings, I feel His displeasure toward me." And yet this woman has spent her adult life in full-time Christian ministry and is an outstanding committed Christian. She is not alone in her feelings. Church historian Richard Lovelace has written that many Christians "below the surface of their lives are guilt-ridden and insecure . . . [and] draw the assurance of their acceptance with God from their sincerity, their past experience of conversion, their recent religious performance or the relative infrequency of their conscious, willful disobedience."[2]

Why is this true? Why do so many believers, including those deeply serious about their Christian commitment, live lives of quiet desperation? One answer is that we have a truncated view of the gospel, tending to see it only as a door we walk through to become a Christian. In this view, the gospel is only for unbelievers. Once you become a Christian, you don't need it anymore except to share with people who are still outside the door. What you need to hear instead are the challenges and how-tos of discipleship.

Another reason for our quiet desperation is that many people have a utilitarian view of the gospel. *What can the gospel do for me?* Some want only the proverbial "fire insurance"—they want the good life now and the good life hereafter. Others are looking for a solution to their problems or a way to a more successful life. This view is aptly illustrated in a breezy church flyer that advertised:

At Valley Church, you

- meet new friends and neighbors
- hear positive, practical messages that uplift you each week on:
  - How to feel good about yourself
  - How to overcome depression
  - How to have a full and successful life
  - Learning to handle your money without it handling you
  - The secrets of successful family living
  - How to overcome stress[3]

This utilitarian view of the gospel is not an isolated instance. A flyer with similar wording was put in my own front door recently.

So, between the challenges of discipleship on one hand and the utilitarian view of the gospel on the other, we fail to see the gospel as the solution to our greatest problem—our guilt, condemnation, and alienation from God. Beyond that, we fail to see it as the basis of our day-to-day acceptance with Him. As a result, many believers live in spiritual poverty.

Some years ago our pastor told an unusual story about a Southern plantation owner who left a $50,000 inheritance to a former slave who had served him faithfully all his life. That was quite a sum of money in those days—perhaps equivalent to half a million dollars today. The lawyer for the estate duly notified the old man of his inheritance and told him that the money had been deposited for him at the local bank. Weeks went by, and the former slave never called for any of his inheritance. Finally, the banker called him in and told him again that he had $50,000 available to draw on at any time. The old man replied, "Sir, do you think I can have fifty cents to buy a sack of cornmeal?" Not having handled money most of his life, this former slave had no comprehension of his wealth. As a result, he was asking for fifty cents when he could easily have had much, much more.

That story illustrates the plight of many Christians today. The apostle Paul wrote of preaching "to the Gentiles the unsearchable riches of Christ" (Ephesians 3:8). Paul was not referring to financial wealth but to the glorious truths of the gospel. To use the figures from the former slave's story, Paul was saying that each of us has $50,000 available to us in the gospel. Yet most of us are hoping we can squeeze out fifty cents' worth. Why is this true? The answer is that we don't understand the riches of the gospel any more than the former slave understood the riches of $50,000.

I grew up in an era and a section of the United States where the realities of heaven and hell were regularly preached. There was no doubt in my mind that there was a hell to shun and a heaven to gain. When finally as a teenager I did trust Christ, my sole objective was just that—to escape hell and go to heaven when I died. Now that, in itself, is of inestimable value, and I wouldn't for a moment minimize the infinite contrast between eternity in heaven and in hell. But that is only part of the gospel. It does not address our relationship with God today.

In our present age, the issue of heaven and hell is irrelevant to most people. Among university students, for example, the open nerve is relationships. The student has had a rotten relationship with his dad and now doesn't get along too well with his roommate. Middle-class working people are concerned about the issues addressed in the church flyer mentioned earlier. The issue of relationships is certainly important, and even some of the subjects on the church flyer are worthy of our attention. But these topics do not begin to explore the "unsearchable riches" Paul was writing about. Paul would probably look at us today and say that we're asking for fifty cents or perhaps a couple of dollars when we have $50,000 in the bank. And he would say that this is because we really don't understand the gospel.

The reality of present-day Christendom is that most professing Christians actually *know* very little of the gospel, let alone understand its implications for their day-to-day lives. My perception is that most of them know just enough gospel to get inside the door of the kingdom. They know nothing of the unsearchable riches of Christ.

So what do we do and where do we begin to grasp a workable understanding of the gospel? That's what this book is intended to address. The word *gospel* means, essentially, "good news." And it is specifically good news about our relationship with God. We all like to receive good news, especially if it addresses some bad news we've just received. If you've just been told that you have cancer, for example, it's good news when the doctor tells you that it is a type that readily responds to treatment.

The gospel is like that. It is the good news that directly addresses the ultimate bad news of our lives. The Bible tells us that we were in deep trouble with God, that we were unrighteous and ungodly. And then it tells us that God's wrath is revealed from heaven "against all the godlessness and wickedness of men." In fact, it tells us that we were by nature objects of God's wrath (see Romans 1:18; 3:10-12; Ephesians 2:3).

Think of that! When you came into the world as a baby,

before you had ever done anything bad, you were an object of God's wrath. We'll find out later why that is true. But for now, that is the bad news.

We are familiar with the well-worn good news/bad news jokes. The bad news comes last, and it's always worse than the good news. But the Bible reverses this sequence. It tells us the bad news that we are in trouble with God, and then it tells us the good news that God has provided a solution that far surpasses our problem. Three times in his letters the apostle Paul paints a grim picture of bad news about us, and then each time he says "*but.*" In effect, he is saying, "Here is the bad news, but here is the Good News as well." And in Paul's message, the Good News always outweighs the bad news.

Take just one of these instances, in Ephesians 2:1-9. After telling us that we were, by nature, objects of wrath, Paul says, *but* now "God, who is rich in mercy," has actually "raised us up with Christ and seated us with him in the heavenly realms." That is surely a dust-to-glory story. What could be a greater contrast than an object of God's wrath seated with His Son in a position of glory?

This good news doesn't begin when we die. It certainly does address that issue, but it also tells us that there is good news for us now. We don't have to feel guilt-ridden and insecure in our relationship with God. We don't have to wonder if He likes us. We can begin each day with the deeply encouraging realization that *I am accepted by God, not on the basis of my personal performance, but on the basis of the infinitely perfect righteousness of Jesus Christ.* We will seek to uncover the depth of meaning in that statement as we work through the coming chapters.

Think again of the story of the former slave. Suppose at the time of coming into his inheritance that he was not only poverty-stricken but also deep in debt for back rent. With his inheritance, he could not only pay off his debt but he could also buy the house. His inheritance far surpasses his debt.

This is the truth of the gospel. We owe an enormous spiritual debt to God—a debt we can't begin to pay. There is no way we can make it good. The gospel tells us that Jesus Christ paid our debt, but it also tells us far more. It tells us that we are no longer enemies and objects of His wrath. We are now His sons and daughters, heirs with Jesus Christ of all His unsearchable riches. This is the good news of the gospel.

Why did the apostle Paul develop at such length the bad news of our situation? We can't begin to appreciate the good news of the gospel until we see our deep need. Most people, even people who have already become believers, have never given much thought to how desperate our condition is outside of Christ. Few people ever think about the dreadful implications of being under the wrath of God. And most of all, none of us even begins to realize how truly sinful we are.

Jesus once told a story about a king's servant who owed his master ten thousand talents (see Matthew 18:21-35). One talent was equal to about twenty years' wages for a working man. Ten thousand talents then would have been around two hundred thousand years' wages—an amount so huge it would have been impossible to pay.

Why would Jesus use such an unrealistically large amount when He knew that in real life it would have been impossible for a king's servant to accumulate such a debt? Jesus was fond of using hyperbole to make His point. In the context of the story, that immense sum represents a spiritual debt that every one of us owes to God. It is the debt of our sins. And, for each of us, it is a staggering amount. There is no way we can pay it.

This is what the gospel is all about. Jesus paid our debt to the full. But He did far more than relieve us of debt. He also purchased for us an eternal inheritance worth infinitely more than the $50,000 the ex-slave inherited. That's why Paul wrote of the "unsearchable riches of Christ." And God wants us to enjoy those unsearchable riches in the here and now, even in the midst of difficult and discouraging circumstances.

The purpose of this book is to explore those unsearchable riches. To appreciate them, however, we need to look briefly at our sinful condition. Though we live in a time when people don't like to talk about sin, only those who understand to some degree the enormity of their spiritual debt can begin to appreciate what Christ did for them at the cross. Without some heartfelt conviction of our sin, we can have no serious feeling of personal interest in the gospel. What's more, this conviction should actually grow throughout our Christian lives. In fact, one sign of spiritual growth is an increased awareness of our sinfulness.

One of the older writers on the subject of the gospel wrote,

> "The best preparation for the study of this doctrine [that is, of the truth of the gospel] is—neither great intellectual ability nor much scholastic learning—but a conscience impressed with a sense of our actual condition as sinners in the sight of God."[4]

In the next chapter we will look at our sinful condition so as to better prepare us to explore those unsearchable riches we have in Christ.

CHAPTER TWO

WHY THE CROSS?

The death of Jesus Christ was the most remarkable event in all history. Centuries before it occurred it was predicted in amazing detail by various Old Testament prophets. And the supernatural phenomena that accompanied the actual event dramatically set it apart from all other deaths before and after.

The Scriptures tell us that during the crucifixion the bright midday sun was totally obscured from high noon until 3 P.M., so that the whole land was plunged into darkness. At the precise moment of His death the thick curtain in the Jewish temple, which set apart the Most Holy Place (the inner room where God symbolically dwelt), was ripped from top to bottom by an invisible hand. An earthquake split the rocks and broke open nearby tombs. Dead people were raised to life and came out of the tombs, later appearing to people in Jerusalem (see Matthew 27:45,51-53).

Three days after His death Jesus arose from the dead and, over a period of forty days, appeared to His disciples on numerous occasions—at one time, to five hundred at once. At the end of that time the apostles saw Him taken up from their sight into a cloud from which He ascended into heaven.

Today, some two thousand years after Christ's death, the cross is the universally recognized symbol of the Christian faith.

It plays a prominent role in the architectural design or furnishings of many church buildings. Christian chaplains in the armed forces wear it on their uniforms as the badge of their office. It has been stylized into various articles of jewelry and is often set with precious stones. Many times such jewelry is worn simply for its beauty by people who have no idea of its significance.

At the time of Christ's death, however, the cross was an instrument of incredible horror and shame. It was a most wretched and degrading punishment, inflicted only on slaves and the lowliest of people. If free men were at any time subjected to crucifixion for great crimes such as treason or insurrection, the sentence could not be executed until they were put in the category of slaves by degradation and their freedom taken away by flogging.[1]

What are we to make of all this? Why was Christ's death such an amazing event in itself? And how could it be that the eternal Son of God, by whom all things were created and for whom all things were created (see Colossians 1:15-16), would end up in His human nature dying one of the most cruel and humiliating deaths ever devised by man?

We know that Jesus' death on the cross did not take Him by surprise. He continually predicted it to His disciples. (See Luke 18:31-33 for one example.) And with His impending crucifixion before Him, Jesus Himself said, "What shall I say? 'Father, save me from this hour'? No, it was for this very reason I came to this hour" (John 12:27). Jesus said He came to die.

But why? Why did Jesus come to die? The apostles Paul and Peter give us the answer in clear, concise terms. Paul wrote, "Christ died for our sins according to the Scriptures," and Peter wrote, "For Christ died for sins once for all, the righteous for the unrighteous, to bring you to God" (1 Corinthians 15:3; 1 Peter 3:18).

Christ died for our sins. Jesus Christ, the eternal Son of God, took upon Himself a human nature and died a horrible death on our behalf. That is the reason for the cross. He suffered what we should have suffered. He died in our place to pay the penalty for our sins.

ADAM'S SIN

We will never understand the cross until we begin to understand something of the nature and depth of our sin. And to understand that, we must go all the way back to the Garden of Eden.

When God placed Adam and Eve in the garden, He imposed a simple prohibition on them. They were not to eat from the tree of the knowledge of good and evil. Why did God not impose some restriction such as, "You shall not steal" or "You shall not murder"? The answer is that God had created Adam and Eve in His image (see Genesis 1:27), which includes, among other things, His moral image. In other words, Adam and Eve were created morally perfect. They were completely sinless and thus did not need moral restrictions placed on them.

God, however, purposed to test their obedience, so He imposed one restriction on them: They were not to eat of the forbidden tree. There was nothing inherently evil about that tree. God could have selected any tree of the garden. Nor was obedience difficult. Many kinds of trees in the garden were pleasing to the eye and good for food. An easier test of Adam and Eve is difficult to imagine. Abstention from the forbidden fruit involved no hardship, no inconvenience, just simple obedience.

Yet when the Serpent questioned God's goodness and truthfulness, Eve capitulated and so did Adam. In that instance they lost the moral image of God; they were no longer perfectly holy. They began to sin immediately, Adam blaming God ("The woman you put here with me . . . ") as well as Eve, and Eve blaming the Serpent. In theological terms their disobedience and consequent loss of God's moral image is known as the *Fall.*

The fall of Adam and the loss of God's moral image resulted not only in guilt, but also in moral depravity or corruption. Now his will, which had been totally responsive to God's will, was biased toward evil. Theologians refer to this persistent bent to evil as *original sin,* an internal drive rooted in the perversity of fallen human nature. Paul called it the *sinful nature* (called the *flesh* in some Bible translations).

The consequences of Adam and Eve's sin went far beyond their own banishment from the garden and the presence of God. God had appointed Adam as the federal head or legal representative of the entire human race. Consequently his fall brought guilt and depravity on all his descendants. That is, all people (except Jesus) after Adam and Eve are born with a sinful nature. David spoke of this fact when he said in Psalm 51:5, "Surely I was sinful at birth, sinful from the time my mother conceived me." David's sinfulness while still in his mother's womb was not in acts of sin committed. He was referring to his sinful nature acquired at conception.

The apostle Paul explained it like this: "Therefore, just as sin entered the world through one man, and death through sin, and in this way death came to all men, because all sinned" (Romans 5:12). Note that Paul's sentence appears to be broken off before he finished his thought. What did Paul mean in saying that "all sinned"? We could easily assume that he was speaking of the individual sins of each of us, but that is not what he had in mind. Rather he was speaking of the fact that Adam was the legal representative of all his descendants. In that sense, what he did, we did. Therefore the consequences of his sin, in terms of both guilt and original sin, fell on all of us.

In Romans 5:18-19, Paul wrote that "the result of one tres-pass was condemnation for all men" and that "through the dis-obedience of the one man the many were made sinners." It is clear in Paul's theology that Adam was appointed by God to act on behalf of all his posterity. That is why you and I, like David, were born with original sin, and why we were by nature objects of God's wrath.

OUR SIN

The story goes downhill from Adam. Since we all have a corrupt sinful nature, we aggravate our condition by our own individual sins. Every day we sin, both consciously and unconsciously, both willfully and unintentionally. We evangelical believers gen-erally abstain from the grosser sins of society; in fact, we tend to sit in judgment of those who practice such things. But beneath the surface of our own lives we tolerate all kinds of "refined" sins such as selfishness, covetousness, pride, resentment, envy, jealousy, self-righteousness, and a critical spirit toward others.

Beyond that, we seldom think about the words of Jesus that the greatest commandment is to "'love the Lord your God with all your heart and with all your soul and with all your mind.' . . . And the second is like it: 'Love your neighbor as yourself'" (Matthew 22:37,39).

Have you ever thought about what it means to love God with all your heart, soul, and mind? I don't think any of us can fully plumb the depths of that commandment, but here are some obvious aspects:

- Your love for God transcends all other desires (see Exodus 20:3).

- Like David, you long to gaze upon His beauty and seek fellowship with Him (see Psalm 27:4).
- You rejoice in meditating on His Word, and, like Jesus, you rise early to pray (see Psalm 119:97, Mark 1:35).
- You always delight to do His will, regardless of how difficult it may be (see Psalm 40:8, NASB).
- A regard for His glory governs and motivates *everything* you do—your eating and drinking, your working and playing, your buying and selling, your reading and speaking—and, dare I mention it, even your driving (see 1 Corinthians 10:31).
- You are never discouraged or frustrated by adverse circumstances because you are confident God is working all things together for your good (see Romans 8:28).
- You recognize His sovereignty in every event of your life and consequently receive both success and failure from His hand (see 1 Samuel 2:7; Psalm 75:6-7).
- You are always content because you know He will never leave you or forsake you (see Hebrews 13:5).
- The first petition in the Lord's Prayer, "hallowed be your name," is the most important prayer you pray (see Matthew 6:9).

This description of the Great Commandment is obviously incomplete, but it is sufficient to show us all how woefully short we come in obeying it.

Now let's take a look at what Jesus called the second commandment: Love your neighbor as yourself. Among other things this would mean:

- You cherish for your neighbors the very same love that you bear toward yourself.

- In your dealings with them you never show selfishness, irritability, peevishness, or indifference.
- You take a genuine interest in their welfare and seek to promote their interests, honor, and well-being.
- You never regard them with a feeling of prideful superiority, nor do you ever talk about their failings.
- You never resent any wrongs they do to you, but instead are always ready to forgive.
- You always treat them as you would have them treat you.
- To paraphrase 1 Corinthians 13:4-5, you are always patient and kind, never envious or boastful, never proud or rude, never self-seeking. You are not easily angered and you keep no record, even in your mind, of wrongs done to you.[2]

Do you begin to grasp some of the implications of what it means to obey these two commandments? Most of us don't even think about them in the course of a day, let alone aspire to obey them. Instead we content ourselves with avoiding major outward sins and performing accepted Christian duties. And yet Jesus said that all the Law and the Prophets hang on these two commandments.

Even in the so-called gross sins, we often resort to euphemisms to mitigate their severity. I sat with some friends across the table from a Christian leader who said, "I have had an affair." Of course we all knew what he meant, but I later wished I had had the presence of mind to say to him, "Bob, look me in the eye and say, 'I have committed adultery.'" We need to call sin what the Bible calls it and not soften it with modern expressions borrowed from our culture.

To probe even deeper, we must realize that our fallen sinful nature affects and pollutes everything we do. Our very best deeds are stained with sin. Because of this, our acts of obedience fall so far short of perfection, defiled as they are by remaining sin, that they are but as "filthy rags" (Isaiah 64:6) when compared with the righteousness God's Law requires.

If we limit our attention to single sins, to the neglect of our sinful nature, we will never discover how deeply infected with sin we really are. When David prayed that memorable prayer of Psalm 51, after he had committed adultery with Bathsheba and had her husband murdered, he traced his heinous actions back to their original cause—his sinful nature acquired in his mother's womb.

You might be thinking by this time, "Why devote so much attention to sin? It just makes me feel guilty. I thought you were going to tell us about the unsearchable riches of Christ." My reason is to cause us all to realize we have no place to hide. In our relationship with God we cannot plead our Christian duties, as helpful as they may be, or our external morality, as exemplary as it may be. Instead we must confess with Ezra that "our sins are higher than our heads and our guilt has reached to the heavens" (Ezra 9:6).

Furthermore, even a deep, penetrating sense of our sinfulness does not do justice to the reality of our predicament. Our need is not to be measured by our own sense of need, but by what God had to do to meet that need. Our situation was so desperate that only the death of His own Son on a cruel and shameful cross was sufficient to resolve the problem.

Many people erroneously think that God can just forgive our sins because He is a loving God. Nothing could be further from the truth. The cross speaks to us not only about our sin but about God's holiness.

GOD'S HOLINESS

When we think of God's holiness we usually think of His infinite moral purity. That is correct, but there is more to it than that. The basic meaning of the word *holy* is "separate," and when used of God it means, among other things, that He is eternally separate from any degree of sin. He does not sin Himself and He cannot abide or condone sin in His moral creatures. He is not like the proverbial indulgent grandfather who winks at or ignores the mischievous disobedience of his grandson.

Instead the Scriptures teach us that God's holiness responds to sin with immutable and eternal hatred. To put it plainly, God hates sin. The psalmist said, "The arrogant cannot stand in your presence; you hate all who do wrong," and "God is a righteous judge, a God who expresses his wrath every day" (Psalm 5:5; 7:11). Thus we see that God always hates sin and inevitably expresses His wrath against it.

The cross, then, is an expression of God's wrath toward sin as well as His love to us. It expresses His holiness in His determination to punish sin, even at the cost of His Son. And it expresses His love in sending His Son to bear the punishment we so justly deserved.

So in answer to the question, "Why the cross?" we must say God's holiness demanded it as punishment for our sins, and God's love provided it to save us from our sins. We cannot begin to understand the true significance of the cross unless we understand something of the holiness of God and the depth of our sin. And it is a continuing sense of the imperfection of our obedience, arising from the constant presence and remaining power of indwelling sin, that drives us more and more as believers to an absolute dependence on the grace of God given to us through His Son, our Lord Jesus Christ.

As we next consider the work of Christ for us, we need to keep in mind our sin that necessitated it. For it is only against the dark backdrop of our sinfulness that we can see the glory of the cross shining forth in all its brilliance and splendor. And, as we gaze upon the glory of the cross, we will also discover that Christ, in His great work for us, not only resolved our sin problem, but also secured for us those "unsearchable riches" that I referred to in the first chapter.

CHAPTER THREE

THE PLEASURE OF OBEDIENCE

If you grew up in a family of several siblings, you can easily remember instances of so-called sibling rivalry. Sometimes you were the victim, sometimes the instigator; but in all cases, there were sinful actions and sinful reactions. Even if you were an only child, or one of two children (as I was), you can likely recall hurtful interactions with your friends. None of us grew up sinless. Even before we heard the word *sin,* we were sinning on a daily basis, just within the confines of our own families.

Jesus grew up in a large family. Matthew records the names of four half-brothers: James, Joseph, Simon, and Judas. Then he speaks of "all his sisters" (Matthew 13:55-56). The word *all* has to denote at least three sisters, perhaps more. So Jesus grew up in a family of four brothers and several sisters, all of whom had sinful natures. Yet in the midst of that situation Jesus never sinned. He never grew impatient with any of His brothers or sisters, never acted out of spite, never retaliated when one of them wronged Him. He was absolutely sinless in every respect, both in His nature and in His behavior.

As He grew into the teenage years, Jesus never once, even in His mind, succumbed to the many temptations of adolescence, such as pride, lust, envy, or covetousness. He was infinitely more than a model teenager. He was sinless.

As an adult He faced the furious onslaught of Satan's temptations in the desert and successfully withstood each of them (see Matthew 4:1-11). Toward the end of His life, in one of His many confrontations with His chief antagonists, the Jewish religious leaders, He could unself-consciously and without any pretentiousness say, "I always do what pleases [the Father]" (John 8:29). Such a claim must include not only Jesus' outward actions and speech, but also His inward thoughts (see Psalm 139:1-4). Even more important, it must include His motives, for God not only knows our thoughts but understands our motives as well (see 1 Chronicles 28:9; 1 Corinthians 4:5).

A little later in the same confrontation Jesus asked, "Can any of you prove me guilty of sin?" (John 8:46). Jesus dared His critics to name a single sin He had committed, knowing full well how eager they would have been to do so if it were possible. Perhaps just as convincing was the fact that He did not hesitate to assert His sinlessness in the presence of the twelve disciples, who had lived and ministered with Him twenty-four hours a day for three years, who heard and saw virtually everything He said and did.

There is an old story about a little boy who insisted on standing up on a pew during the church service. After several admonishments his mother severely threatened him if he stood up one more time. As he sat squirming on the pew he whispered to his mother, "I'm sitting down on the outside, but I'm standing up on the inside." All of us should be able to identify with the little boy to some degree. There are times when our inward desires do not match our outward conduct. We act very proper on the outside, but sin in our hearts. This was never the case with Jesus. Through one of the messianic psalms He could say, "I desire to do your will, O my God; your law is within my heart" (Psalm 40:8). He not only perfectly obeyed the Law of

God, He always desired to do so. In fact, most other Bible translations render Psalm 40:8 as, "I *delight* to do your will, O my God" (emphasis added). We could say that Jesus not only *desired* to do God's will, He also *delighted* in doing it. Once He even said, "My food . . . is to do the will of him who sent me" (John 4:34).

If we think about it, we realize that obedience that is not delighted in is not perfect obedience. Yet that was the quality of obedience Jesus rendered throughout His life, from birth to death. It is no wonder that at the beginning of His ministry and again toward the end of it, a voice came from heaven saying, "This is my Son, whom I love; with him I am well pleased" (Matthew 3:17; 17:5). What, however, is the significance to us of His perfect obedience?

ACTIVE AND PASSIVE OBEDIENCE

The apostle John wrote that Jesus' undergarment "was seamless, woven in one piece from top to bottom" (John 19:23). That is the way we should view Christ's work on our behalf. Though of necessity we must look at His work one part at a time, keep in mind that each part is a thread of a seamless garment comprising His entire life, death, and resurrection.

The seamless-garment perspective must guide us as we consider the two overall aspects of Christ's work: His life and His death. In recent years Christians have tended to focus almost exclusively on the death of Christ to the neglect of His sinless life. For the most part Jesus' life of perfect obedience has been seen only as a necessary precondition to His death. The truth is, however, Jesus not only died for us, He also lived for us. That is, all that Christ did in both His life and death, He did in our place as our substitute.

33

Theologians have historically used two adjectives, *active* and *passive,* to distinguish the two major aspects of Christ's obedience. In this context these words do not have their ordinary grammatical meaning (*active* describing actions we do and *passive* describing actions done to us). Neither are they intended to denote two periods of Jesus' history, namely His life and His death. Rather, they refer to the two works of Christ in regard to God's Law. The Law contains both precepts and penalties. The precepts are to be fully obeyed, and the penalties are imposed for the least infraction of the precepts.

The Law of God set forth in Scripture is a transcript of God's own moral nature. It is the Law that was fully imprinted on Adam's heart as part of his being created in God's image. It is the same Law that the apostle Paul said is still written on people's hearts regardless of how obscured it may now be (see Romans 2:12-16). It is a universal law applicable to all people of all times. When the apostle Paul wrote that Christ was "born under law" (Galatians 4:4), he was referring to this universal moral will of God. Jesus was born under the Law because He came to perfectly obey it in our place. He came to do what we, because of our sinful nature, could not do. It is this perfect obedience to the moral will of God that constitutes His *active* obedience.

There is, however, another significant dimension to Jesus' obedience. As our representative, He not only was obligated to obey the precepts of the Law, but to suffer its penalty for our violation of it. This obligation He freely assumed in obedience to the Father's will. So He *actively* obeyed the Father's universal moral will, which we call the Law of God, and He *passively* obeyed the Father's specific will for Him, namely to suffer the penalty for our sin. The writer of Hebrews referred to this specific will of God for Jesus when he wrote, "And by that will, we have been made holy through the sacrifice of the body of Jesus Christ once for all" (Hebrews 10:10).

So it is the suffering of Christ in our place that constitutes His *passive* obedience. But we should not limit His suffering just to the hours He hung on the cross. It actually began at His incarnation when He laid aside His divine glory and assumed a human nature subject to the same physical weaknesses and infirmities we are exposed to.

He was born into a poor family in a nation under the heel of a foreign empire. His first crib was an animal's feed trough. As a sinless child in a family of sinful brothers and sisters He must often have suffered at their hands. The Scriptures specifically tell us that during His three years of public ministry His brothers did not believe in Him, and on at least one occasion mocked Him (see John 7:1-5). He was misunderstood, criticized, and harassed by the Jewish religious leaders. In the words of the prophet Isaiah, "He was despised and rejected by men, a man of sorrows, and familiar with suffering" (Isaiah 53:3).

In Galatians 6:7 the apostle Paul stated a universal moral principle: "A man reaps what he sows." Sin has consequences, both spiritual and temporal. Jesus, in a sense, reaped what we have sown.[1] His entire life was one of suffering obedience and obedient suffering. He suffered throughout His life and He was obedient throughout His life, even in the face of the suffering He endured. Of course, His suffering reached its climax on the cross, but even there we see His perfect obedience when he prayed the night before, "My Father, if it is possible, may this cup be taken from me. Yet not as I will, but as you will" (Matthew 26:39).

In fact, Jesus was active even in His death. According to Hebrews 9:14, He "offered himself unblemished to God." He functioned both as high priest and sacrifice. Further, even before His death He said, "I lay down my life for the sheep. . . . No one takes it from me, but I lay it down of my own accord"

(John 10:15,18). In one sense, Jesus was as active on the cross as He had been in His life up to the cross.

It is true, however, that the major focus of biblical teaching on the work of Christ concerns His death. That is because of the terrible damage that sin did to our relationship with God. It violated His justice, aroused His wrath, stirred up His enmity, and brought us under His curse. Moreover, it resulted in our becoming spiritually dead, in bondage to Satan, and under the dominion of sin (see Ephesians 2:1-3). In subsequent chapters we will see how Christ's death for us addressed each of these terrible consequences. But before we discuss that, we must grasp one more essential truth in order to appreciate something of the unsearchable riches of Christ.

UNION WITH CHRIST

On several occasions in this chapter I have referred to Jesus living and dying in our place. That is, as our representative, He assumed our obligation to perfectly obey the Law of God and fulfilled it completely. We call this His *active obedience*. Then He also assumed our liability for disobedience and paid that liability to the full. This we call His *passive obedience*. The point I want to stress at this time, however, is that He assumed *our* obligation and liability, obeying and suffering in *our* place.

How can this be? How can Jesus take our place both in obeying God's Law and in suffering the consequences of disobeying it? How can the innocent suffer for the guilty? How can consistently disobedient people be treated as if they were perfectly obedient?

Jesus was appointed by God the Father as our legal representative. We saw in chapter 2 that Adam was appointed as the federal head or legal representative of the entire human race (except for Jesus, of course). Because of this we all suffered the consequences of his disobedience. In the same manner Jesus was appointed the legal representative of all His people—that is, of all who would ever trust in Him. This is the point Paul was making when he wrote in Romans 5:19, "For just as through the disobedience of the one man the many were made sinners, so also through the obedience of the one man the many will be made righteous."

This legal representation, called *federal headship* by theologians, is the basis upon which the life and death of Christ become effective for us. There would be absolutely no benefit to us if Jesus merely lived and died as a private person. It is only because He lived and died as our representative that His work becomes beneficial to us.

Over and over again in Paul's writings he uses the expressions *in Christ, in Him,* and *in the Lord.* This is his way of referring to what is called our *union with Christ,* which means that in a spiritual but nevertheless real way we are united to Christ, both legally and vitally. *Legal union* refers to what we have already considered—that Christ was appointed by God to be our representative in His life and in His death. It is the basis upon which we can say that Christ lived in our place and died in our place as our representative and our substitute.

It is this legal union that the apostle Paul had in view when he wrote that we were crucified with Christ, that we died with Him, were buried with Him, were made [spiritually] alive with Him, and will ultimately be united with Him in His resurrection (see Galatians 2:20; Romans 6:4-5,10; Ephesians 2:5). In other words, all that Christ did in His life and death is effective for us because we are legally united to Him. Therefore, we can accurately say that when Jesus lived a perfect life, we lived a perfect life. When He died on the cross to suffer the penalty of sin, we died on the cross. All that Jesus did, we did, because of our legal union with Him.

Just as the guilt of Adam's sin was *charged* to us because he was our legal representative, so the sinless life and sin-bearing death of Christ was *credited* to us because He was the legal representative of all who trust in Him. It is crucial that we grasp this truth because it is the sole basis upon which Christ's entire work in His life and death becomes effective for us. It is the sole basis upon which He becomes our substitute and upon which we become entitled to those unsearchable riches in Him.

This does not mean that Christ's work is effective for everyone, because not everyone is in union with Him. We are united to Christ by faith—that is, by trusting in Him as our Savior. But the moment we trust in Christ, we become partakers of and beneficiaries of all that He did in both His life and death.

A few paragraphs ago, I said that we are united to Christ both legally *and* vitally. In chapter 15 we will consider what it means to be united to Christ vitally. For now, we can distinguish these two aspects of our union with Christ this way: Our legal union with Christ entitles us to all that Christ did *for* us as He acted in our place, as our substitute. Our vital union with Christ is the means by which He works *in* us by His Holy Spirit. The legal union refers to His *objective* work outside of us that is credited to us through faith. The vital union refers to His *subjective* work in us, which is also realized through faith as we rely on His Spirit to work in and through us.

Though our union with Christ has two aspects, it is *one* union. We cannot have legal union without also having vital union. If through faith we lay hold of what Christ did for us, we will also begin to experience His working in us.

Have you ever thought about the wonderful truth that

Christ lived His perfect life in your place and on your behalf? Has it yet gripped you that when God looks at you today He sees you clothed in the perfect, sinless obedience of His Son? And that when He says, "This is my Son, whom I love; with Him I am well pleased," He includes you in that warm embrace? The extent to which we truly understand this is the extent to which we will begin to enjoy those unsearchable riches that are found in Christ.

CHAPTER FOUR

JUSTICE SATISFIED

The two young men pulled up alongside a car stopped at a traffic signal. On the prowl for someone to rape, they saw a lovely young woman in the car, just the kind of target they were looking for. Following the woman to an apartment complex, they seized her, took her to an empty schoolground, and both raped her. Realizing she could identify them if left alive, they decided to kill her in a most demeaning and horrible manner.

Back at the apartment complex some residents had heard the young woman scream as she was being abducted, noted the license number of the men's car, and notified the police. Within a few hours the two men were apprehended and the murder knife, still covered with blood, was found in their car.

The entire community was deeply stirred by the heinous nature of such a crime, committed on a randomly chosen victim just about to graduate from the local university. Because of the brutality of the crime and the unquestioned guilt of the young men, both of whom confessed, the district attorney asked for the death penalty.

The men were of course tried separately. The defense lawyer, while acknowledging the alleged actions of the first man to be tried, sought to prove that he was unduly influenced by the second man and thus not legally guilty. The jury was unconvinced and returned a verdict of guilty on all counts, but a three-judge panel that was convened to determine whether the man should receive the death penalty or life imprisonment failed to reach the unanimous decision required for death.

Now the community was outraged at the failure of the judicial panel to sentence the man to death. Regardless of what one may think of the death penalty, the people in that community felt that justice had been violated. They believed the man did not receive the penalty he deserved. They wanted justice, not mercy.

This is the way most of us tend to view justice, especially in a case where a terrible crime has been committed. We want to see justice done. But what about the guilty party? He hopes for mercy or even a miscarriage of justice. He doesn't want to see justice done. He wants as light a sentence as possible, or perhaps even to be declared not guilty.

GOD'S JUSTICE

Now consider our relationship with God. The Bible tells us that all of us will eventually face judgment before a holy and just God (see, for example, Hebrews 9:27). As we think of that inevitable day, what do we want? Do we want to see justice done, or do we want mercy? Except for the most arrogantly self-righteous among us, we would all hope for mercy. Here, however, is our dilemma: God's justice is certain and it is inflexible.

God's justice is certain. In 2 Thessalonians 1:6-8 the apostle Paul says, "God is just: He *will* pay back. . . . He *will* punish those who do not know God" (emphasis added). And again in Romans 12:19, he writes, "'It is mine to avenge; I *will* repay,' says the Lord" (emphasis added). Though God's justice is often delayed, it is nonetheless certain.

God's justice is also inflexible. *Justice* may be defined as rendering to everyone according to one's due. Justice means we get *exactly* what we deserve—nothing more, nothing less. In our human system of justice a tension often exists between justice and mercy. Sometimes one prevails at the expense of the other. But there is no tension with God. Justice always prevails. God's justice must be satisfied; otherwise His moral government would be undermined.

God does not exalt His mercy at the expense of His justice. And in order to maintain His justice, all sin without exception must be punished. Contrary to popular opinion, with God there is no such thing as mere forgiveness. There is only justice.

Let's pursue the idea of mere forgiveness a little further. In the case of the young men in our story, the second one was sentenced to die. Suppose the governor of the state did not believe in the death penalty and issued a full pardon to the man. Although the governor would have the authority to do that, he would be subverting justice. Now the community would be even more incensed. They might even try to pressure the legislature to impeach the governor for such a grave miscarriage of justice.

Yet this is what most people expect God to do. They think that God will somehow relax His inflexible justice and pardon all of us by mere sovereign prerogative. But God, by the perfection of His nature, cannot do that. God cannot exalt one of His glorious attributes, such as mercy, at the expense of another attribute—in this case His justice. Justice must be satisfied. What is the solution, then, to our own personal dilemma? What are we to expect when we stand before God's bar of judgment?

JESUS' SATISFACTION

The answer to our dilemma lies in the cross. Through His death on the cross Jesus fully satisfied the justice of God on our behalf. In chapter 3 we saw that Jesus fully satisfied the demands of God's Law by completely obeying it in its most exacting requirements. And we also saw that He did this in our place as our representative. Therefore, God regards all who trust in Christ as having fully obeyed His Law in all its demands. We can correctly say that in God's sight, when Jesus perfectly obeyed God's Law, we perfectly obeyed His Law.

However, the Law contains both precepts and penalties: precepts to be obeyed, and penalties for the least failure to do so. Penalty is an essential element of any law, or even of an athletic contest. There can be no law, or even rules of a game, to which penal sanction is not attached. It would be virtually useless, for example, to set a twenty-mile-per-hour speed limit in a school zone if there were no penalty attached to the law.

We have already seen in chapter 2 that all of us have failed miserably to obey God's Law. We disobeyed in Adam, and we have every day of our lives disobeyed in our own persons. Therefore all of us stand condemned before God's Law, fully liable to its curse and punishment. But just as Jesus fully obeyed God's Law in our place, so He suffered its full penalty in our place.

In the same way that Adam was our representative in the garden, so Christ was our representative on the cross. He bore the full brunt of God's justice that we should have borne. He received the full punishment we should have received. As the Scripture says, "But *he* was pierced for *our* transgressions, *he* was crushed for *our* iniquities; the punishment that brought *us* peace was upon *him,* and by *his* wounds *we* are healed" (Isaiah 53:5, emphasis added).

Through His representative union with us, Jesus assumed our obligation to perfectly obey the Law of God and obeyed it to the letter. Through that same union Jesus assumed our liability for not obeying the Law and paid that liability to the utmost. He fully and completely satisfied the justice of God on our behalf as our substitute.

Therefore everyone who has trusted in Christ as Savior can say, "God's justice toward me is satisfied." In our judicial system, when a sentence has been fully served, justice is satisfied. If someone who has been sentenced to ten years in prison fully serves that time, he can walk out of prison a completely free person. Justice no longer has a claim on him. It has been satisfied.

As believers we must steadily keep in mind that Christ has satisfied the justice of God on our behalf. Never again should we fear the retributive justice of God. Yet many believers do live under a sense of fear of God's justice. We know we sin continually, and sometimes the painful awareness of our sin almost overwhelms us. At such times we still are prone to view God as our judge meting out absolute justice. We fail to grasp by faith the fact that Christ Jesus has fully satisfied God's justice for us.

One morning in my private devotions I was reflecting on my sin, which for some reason seemed particularly painful to me that day. In my discouragement I blurted out, "God, You would be perfectly just in sending me to hell." Immediately on the heel of those words, though, came this thought: "No, You wouldn't, because Jesus satisfied Your justice for me."

This is the stand we must take as believers. We must not allow the accusations of Satan or the condemning indictments of our consciences to bring us under a sense of God's unrequited justice. Instead, we should by faith lay hold of the wonderful truth that God's justice has been satisfied for us by our Lord Jesus Christ.

JUSTICE AND MERCY

The death of Jesus was a complete and full satisfaction of divine justice for all who trust in Him. At the cross there is no tension between justice and mercy; instead, they meet in full harmony. Justice suffers no violence and mercy has full expression. In fact, not only has justice suffered no violence, it has been honored and magnified. It has exacted its penalty and been completely satisfied. Therefore, as believers we can rejoice in the abundant mercy of God through Christ, while at the same time fully honoring the inviolate nature of His holy justice.

At the conclusion of his most extended discourse on the mercy of God, the apostle Paul cries out, "Oh, the depth of the riches of the wisdom and knowledge of God! How unsearchable his judgments, and his paths beyond tracing out" (Romans 11:33). Only God's infinite wisdom and superabundant love could devise such a plan that both satisfies His justice and meets our desperate need for mercy. Let us then join Paul in exalting the mercy and wisdom of God as by faith we lay hold of this aspect of the unsearchable riches of Christ.

CHAPTER FIVE

THE EMPTY CUP

—⸺⸻—

I n the Garden of Gethsemane Jesus prayed, "My Father, if it is possible, may this cup be taken from me. Yet not as I will, but as you will." A little later, at His arrest, He said to Peter, "Put your sword away! Shall I not drink the cup the Father has given me?" (Matthew 26:39; John 18:11). It is obvious that the cup was very much on Jesus' mind that night. The question is, then, what was in the cup?

We generally associate Jesus' cup with His crucifixion. We assume that when He prayed that the cup might be taken away, He was asking that, if possible, He might be spared from that horrible and demeaning death on the cross. There is truth in that assumption, and certainly the cup was connected with the crucifixion. But we still have not answered the question: What was in the cup?

In both the Old and New Testaments the cup of God is a reference to His judgment. For example, in Psalm 75:8 we read,

In the hand of the LORD is a cup
full of foaming wine mixed with spices;
he pours it out, and all the wicked of the earth
drink it down to its very dregs.

Here we see that the cup that God pours out and that the wicked drink down to its very dregs is the cup of God's judgment. The same basic idea of judgment is expressed in Habakkuk 2:16.

Jeremiah 25:15 is even more specific. In this verse God says, "Take from my hand this cup filled with the wine of my wrath and make all the nations to whom I send you drink it." Here the cup is filled with the wrath of God. (See also Isaiah 51:17,22.)

Finally as Revelation 14:9-10 looks out into the future, it again refers to the cup of God's wrath:

> A third angel followed them and said in a loud voice: "If anyone worships the beast and his image and receives his mark on the forehead or on the hand, he, too, will drink of the wine of God's fury, which has been poured full strength into the cup of his wrath. He will be tormented with burning sulfur in the presence of the holy angels and of the Lamb."

So we see that the cup is a metaphorical expression referring to the judgment of God as expressed in the pouring out of His wrath on sinful nations and people.

THE WRATH OF GOD

This brings us to a difficult subject of the Bible, one that is at worst denied by some scholars and at best ignored by most believers: the wrath of God. Perhaps we shy away from the expression *the wrath of God* because of the violent emotions and destructive behavior that we frequently associate with the word *wrath* when used of sinful human beings. We are reluctant, and rightly so, to attribute that same kind of attitude and activity to God.

I suspect, however, that the more basic reason we avoid or ignore the idea of God's wrath is that we simply don't think of our sinfulness as warranting the degree of judgment inferred by the expression. Frankly, most people don't think they are that bad. A divine reprimand or an occasional slap on the wrist may be needed, most would agree, but the outpouring of divine wrath? That's much too severe.

Perhaps another reason we avoid the subject is that we don't want to think of our nice, decent, but unbelieving neighbors and relatives as still subject to the wrath of God. Unconsciously, then, we adopt the head-in-the-sand philosophy that if we ignore something, it will just go away.

The Bible, however, does not give us that option. Over and over again it asserts that the wrath of God is expressed in both temporal and eternal judgment. Noted New Testament scholar Leon Morris writes, "In the Old Testament more than twenty words are used of the wrath of God," and, "The total number of references to God's wrath [in the Old Testament] exceeds 580."[1]

What about the New Testament? Here again some people like to think that even if the wrath of God is a reality in the Old Testament era, it disappears in the teaching of Jesus, and His love and mercy become the only expressions of God's attitude toward His creatures. Jesus clearly refutes that notion. In John 3:36 He says, "Whoever believes in the Son has eternal life, but whoever rejects the Son will not see life, for God's wrath remains on him."[2] More important than His use of the word *wrath,* however, are His frequent references to hell as the ultimate, eternal expression of God's wrath. (See, for example, Matthew 5:22; 18:9; Mark 9:47; Luke 12:5.)

Turning to the inspired letters of Paul, we read, "The wrath of God is being revealed from heaven against all the godlessness and wickedness of men who suppress the truth by their wickedness" (Romans 1:18). We read of God's wrath being "stored up" for the day of judgment (see Romans 2:5). We learn that we were by nature objects of wrath, and that God's wrath is coming because of sin (see Ephesians 2:3; Colossians 3:6). Finally, the whole tenor of Revelation warns us of the wrath to come. (See Revelation 6:16-17; 14:10; 16:19; and 19:15 for explicit references to God's wrath.)

Having then established the grim reality of God's wrath, and having understood that it is not the same as the uncontrollable passion in human beings associated with that word, how are we to understand the wrath of God? God's wrath arises from His intense, settled hatred of all sin and is the tangible expression of His inflexible determination to punish it. We might say God's wrath is His justice in action, rendering to everyone his just due, which, because of our sin, is always judgment.

But, we may ask, why is God so angry because of our sin? It is because our sin, regardless of how small or insignificant it may seem to us, is essentially an assault on the infinite majesty and sovereign authority of God. Nineteenth-century theologian George Smeaton wrote, "Without [any] of the turbulent emotions found in us, and which betrays human weakness, the supreme Lawgiver, from the perfection of His nature, is *angry at sin*, because it is a violation of His authority, and a wrong to His inviolable majesty" (emphasis his).[3]

It is here that we begin to realize the seriousness of sin. All sin is rebellion against God's authority, a despising of His Law, and a defiance of His commands. W. S. Plumer wrote, "We never see sin aright until we see it as against God. All sin is against God in this sense that it is His Law that is broken, His authority that is despised, His government that is set at naught."[4]

God, by the very perfection of His moral nature, cannot but be angry at sin—not only because of its destructiveness to humans, but, more important, because of its assault on His divine majesty. This is not the mere petulance of an offended deity because His commands are not obeyed. It is rather the necessary response of God to uphold His moral authority in His universe. And though God's wrath does not contain the sinful emotions associated with human wrath, it does contain a fierce intensity arising from His settled opposition to sin and His determination to punish it to the utmost.

THE CUP OF WRATH

This brings us back again to the cup Jesus drank at His crucifixion. What was in the cup? It was the wrath of God. It was the cup of wrath that we should have drunk. Jesus as our representative drank the cup of God's wrath in our place. He drained it to its dregs. He tasted the last drop. And He did it for us as our substitute.

Scripture tells us that while Jesus hung on the cross, darkness came over the land from noon until three o'clock. During those awful three hours Jesus drank the cup of God's wrath in our place. It was toward the end of that time that He cried out, "My God, my God, why have you forsaken me?" (Matthew 27:46).

We do not know all that transpired during those three terrible hours when Jesus endured the wrath of God. Scripture draws a veil over them for the most part. We do know that the physical suffering Jesus endured was only a feeble picture of the suffering of His soul. And part of that suffering was the very real forsakenness by His Father, His utter abandonment by God. The night before, He had been strengthened by divine assistance (see Luke 22:43), but now He was left alone. For our sakes, God turned His back on His own dearly loved Son.

We can perhaps better understand what transpired that day by considering Paul's words in 2 Corinthians 5:21: "God made him who had no sin to be sin for us, so that in him we might become the righteousness of God." Christ is here represented as "made sin" for us by a judicial act of God; that is, by charging the guilt of our sin to Him. He was made sin for us because of the representative union that exists between Him and His people, whereby He assumed the guilt and consequent punishment of our sins. As Isaiah the prophet wrote, "We all, like sheep, have gone astray, each of us has turned to his own way; and the LORD has laid on him the iniquity of us all" (Isaiah 53:6).

Jesus was forsaken by the Father because of our sin. He drank the cup of God's wrath to endure the judgment and punishment that was due to us. As the apostle Peter wrote, "He himself bore our sins in his body on the tree" (1 Peter 2:24). God the Father laid our sins—every one of them—on Christ, and He willingly for our sake bore them on the cross.

However, as we contemplate with wonder Christ being made sin for us, we must always keep in mind the distinction between Christ's sinlessness in His personal being and His sin-bearing in His official liability to God's wrath. He was the sinless sin-bearer. Though He was officially guilty as our representative, He was personally the object of the Father's everlasting love and delight.

Even as Jesus hung on the cross bearing our sins and enduring the full fury of God's wrath, He was at the same time the object of His Father's infinite, eternal love. Should this not make us bow in adoration at such matchless love, that the Father would subject the object of His supreme delight to His unmitigated wrath for our sake?

PROPITIATION? WHAT'S THAT?

The Bible uses a strange word to describe what Christ did for us when He drank the cup of God's wrath in our place: *propitiation*. Actually, if you look for that word in most modern versions of the Bible you will not find it. Because the word is little understood and perhaps difficult to pronounce or spell, modern translators have sought another word or phrase to replace it. For example, the *New International Version* (NIV), the translation used in this book, substitutes *atoning sacrifice*. But *propitiation* is a good word and one that all sincere believers should understand and contemplate with wonder and amazement when it is used to describe the work of Christ for us.

What does *propitiation* mean? A modern dictionary will say that to *propitiate* means "to appease" or "to placate." I find both of these words unsatisfactory because they suggest a mere soothing or softening of the wrath of an offended deity. In addition the word *appease* carries negative baggage, implying an attempt to buy off an aggressor by making concessions, usually at the expense of principle.

The NIV, in the instances where it substitutes the words *atoning sacrifice,* consistently adds a footnote saying, "as the one who would turn aside his wrath, taking away sin."[5] Leon Morris says that this footnote recognizes the true meaning of propitiation.[6] I was still not satisfied, however, because even "turning aside" seems to describe a mere *deflection* of wrath, as in the case of a boxer deflecting a blow from his opponent. In that instance the opponent is disappointed that his blow did not strike its intended target. Obviously, Jesus did more than merely deflect the wrath of God from us.

I believe a word that forcefully captures the essence of Jesus' work of propitiation is the word *exhausted*. Jesus exhausted the wrath of God. It was not merely deflected and prevented from reaching us; it was exhausted. Jesus bore the full, unmitigated brunt of it. God's wrath against sin was unleashed in all its fury on His beloved Son. He held nothing back.

The prophet Isaiah foretold this when he wrote, "yet we considered him *stricken* by God, *smitten* by him, and *afflicted*. But he was *pierced* for our transgressions, he was *crushed* for our iniquities; the *punishment* that brought us peace was upon him, and by his *wounds* we are healed" (Isaiah 53:4-5, emphasis added).

Note the italicized words: *stricken, smitten, afflicted, pierced, crushed, punishment, wounds*. They describe the pouring out of God's wrath on His Son. During those awful hours when Jesus hung on the cross, the cup of God's wrath was completely turned upside down. Christ *exhausted* the cup of God's wrath. For all who trust in Him there is nothing more in the cup. It is empty.

It was the immediate prospect of drinking the cup of God's wrath that caused Jesus such intense agony in the Garden of Gethsemane. That is why the Scriptures say, "And being in anguish, he prayed more earnestly, and his sweat was like drops of blood falling to the ground" (Luke 22:44). That is why as Jesus hung on the cross, He cried out, "My God, my God, why have you forsaken me?"

And then at the end of those terrible hours Jesus again cried out, "It is finished" (John 19:30; see also Mark 15:37).[7] This was not a cry of relief, but a cry of triumph. He had accomplished what He came to do, to save His people from the wrath of God. And He did this, not merely by deflecting it away from us, but by consuming it in His own person.

That is why Paul could write of our being "saved from God's wrath through him" and say that "God did not appoint us to suffer wrath but to receive salvation through our Lord Jesus Christ" (Romans 5:9; 1 Thessalonians 5:9). All who trust in Jesus need never fear the possibility of experiencing the wrath of God. It was exhausted on His Son as He stood in our place, bearing the guilt of our sin. That is what propitiation means.[8]

THE LOVE OF GOD

There is one more important truth we need to consider about Jesus' propitiatory work. It was initiated by the Father because of His great love for us. The apostle John wrote:

> This is how God showed his love among us: He sent
> his one and only Son into the world that we might live
> through him. This is love: not that we loved God, but
> that he loved us and sent his Son as an atoning sacri-
> fice [a propitiation] for our sins. (1 John 4:9-10)

Sometimes the work of Christ is erroneously depicted as a kind and gentle Jesus placating the wrath of a vengeful God, as if Jesus needed to persuade the Father not to pour out His wrath on us. Nothing could be further from the truth. God the Father sent His Son on this great errand of mercy and grace. Though Jesus came voluntarily and gladly, He was sent by the Father.

Scripture consistently affirms the Father's love as the compelling cause of Jesus' great work of atonement. "For God so loved the world that he gave his one and only Son" (John 3:16). "But God demonstrates his own love for us in this: While we were still sinners, Christ died for us" (Romans 5:8).

Note how the wrath of God and the love of God are juxtaposed by Paul in the following Scripture:

> Like the rest [of humankind], we were by nature objects of wrath. But because of his great love for us, God, who is rich in mercy, made us alive with Christ even when we were dead in transgressions—it is by grace you have been saved. (Ephesians 2:3-5)

Herein lies the glory of the cross. Justice and mercy are reconciled; wrath and love are both given full expression—and all of this so that we might experience the unsearchable riches of Christ.

What great humility and gratitude this should produce in us: humility that we were the cause of our Savior's unimaginable suffering, and gratitude that He so willingly and lovingly experienced God's wrath that we might not suffer it ourselves. When I think of Christ's great work of propitiation, I am compelled to sing those grand old words of Isaac Watts:

> When I survey the wondrous cross
> On which the Prince of glory died,
> My richest gain I count but loss,
> And pour contempt on all my pride.

CHAPTER SIX

THE SCAPEGOAT

The deep economic crisis that occurred in Russia soon after the collapse of communism resulted in a new wave of resentment and hostility toward Russian Jews. In times of crisis people look for a scapegoat. In this case, as so frequently in history, the scapegoat was the Jewish people.

A scapegoat is one who is made to bear the blame for the actions of others or for events he did not cause. In Russia, the cause of the crisis was probably a complex matter, centering in the government's inability or unwillingness to transition from a centrally controlled economy to a free market economy. But rather than see themselves as the cause of the problem, key Russian officials blamed the Jews, making them the scapegoat for their own disastrous decisions.

The greatest scapegoat in all of history, however, is the Lord Jesus Christ. The word is never used of Him in the Bible, but it is used of a male goat in the Old Testament sacrificial system, all of which pictured the one great sacrifice of Jesus in His death. Each year the elaborate system of sacrifices inaugurated by God for the Jewish people reached its climax on the great Day of Atonement. On that day two male goats were selected, and the high priest cast lots over them. One was to be killed and its blood sprinkled on and before the mercy seat in the Most Holy

Place where God symbolically dwelt. The death of this goat as a sacrifice to God symbolized our Lord's *propitiatory* sacrifice on the cross for us.

The role of the second goat is described in Leviticus 16:20-22:

> When Aaron has finished making atonement for the Most Holy Place, the Tent of Meeting and the altar, he shall bring forward the live goat. He is to lay both hands on the head of the live goat and confess over it all the wickedness and rebellion of the Israelites—all their sins—and put them on the goat's head. He shall send the goat away into the desert in the care of a man appointed for the task. The goat will carry on itself all their sins to a solitary place; and the man shall release it in the desert.

By laying both hands on the goat's head and confessing over it all the sins of the people, the high priest symbolically transferred those sins to the goat, which then carried them away to a solitary place where it would never be seen again. This goat was called the scapegoat because all the guilt of the people was transferred to it, and it bore their sins away into the desert.

Thus, in the first part of the ritual involving the two goats, the death of the first goat symbolized the means of propitiating the wrath of God through the death of an innocent victim substituted in the sinner's place. The sending away of the second goat set forth the effect of this propitiation, the complete removal of the sins from the presence of the Holy God and from His people.

Since both goats represented Christ, we may say Christ became our scapegoat, bearing the guilt of our sins in His propitiatory sacrifice and by that act bearing them away from the presence of His holy Father.

THE SCAPEGOAT ILLUSTRATED

There are several Old Testament metaphors and colorful expressions that God uses to assure us that, just as the Israelites' sins were *symbolically* carried away by the scapegoat, so our sins have been *literally* carried away by our Lord Jesus Christ. The first of these is Psalm 103:12: "As far as the east is from the west, so far has he removed our transgressions from us."

What is the significance of the expression "as far as the east is from the west"? Probably it was a cultural idiom signifying as great a distance as human vocabulary can express. Practically, it expresses an infinite distance. This is what God has done with our sin. Jesus not only bore our sins on the cross, He carried them away an infinite distance. He removed them from the presence of God and from us forever. Just as the goat symbolically carried away the sins of the Israelites from the presence of God and their presence, so Christ by His death carried away our sins. They are forever removed from God's holy presence. They can no longer bar our access to Him. Now we may enter into His presence with confidence, or as the *King James Version* puts it more strikingly, with *boldness* (see Hebrews 10:19).

A second Scripture that reinforces the message of the scapegoat is Isaiah 38:17, where King Hezekiah said to God, "You have put all my sins behind your back." When something is behind your back you can't see it anymore. It is out of sight. This is God's way of saying to us, through Hezekiah's metaphorical expression, that He has completely dealt with our sin and put it away.

There is an emphatic ring to Hezekiah's words. They suggest

a deliberate, decisive action on God's part. God Himself has put our sins behind His back, and He is not hesitant or reluctant in doing this. He has taken the initiative, and He did so joyfully and gladly. God takes pleasure in putting our sins behind His back because He takes pleasure in the work of His Son.

The question we must ask ourselves is, do we believe this? Do we believe the testimony of Scripture, or do we believe our guilty feelings? Only to the extent we believe God has indeed put our sins behind His back will we be motivated and enabled to effectively deal with those sins in our daily lives.

In Isaiah 43:25, God says, "I, even I, am he who blots out your transgressions, for my own sake, and remembers your sins no more." Here God uses two absolute terms to assure us of the complete removal of our sins: *blots out* and *remembers no more.* To blot out something is to remove it from the record. An event in the life of a Canadian friend of mine can help us see what God did when He blotted out our sins. (Although I told of this incident in an earlier book, *Transforming Grace,* it so powerfully illustrates what *blots out* means that it bears repeating.)

Because of a teenage prank, my friend was convicted of a felony, but received what is called in Canada a *Queen's pardon.* Years later, when he was routinely investigated for past criminal activity, the response came back, "We have no record of this person." His record has not just been marked "pardoned," it has been completely removed from the file and destroyed. It's as if my friend had never been convicted. There is no permanent legal stain hanging over his head. There is no chance that the offense will ever arise to haunt him in the future.

This is what God has done for us. He has *blotted out* our sins, removing them from His record. He has done more than wipe the slate clean. He has thrown away the slate!

Not only has God blotted out our sins, He further says He

remembers them no more. Someone has helpfully pointed out the difference between forgetting and not remembering. Forgetting is something we do because of our fallible minds. We forget to pick up something at the store, or we forget where we laid our car keys. Obviously, God does not forget as we do.

On the other hand, to not remember is to choose not to bring something to one's mind ever again. And God has promised never to remember our sins, never to bring them to His mind again. What an overwhelming thought! What joy this should bring to our hearts. Think of some of your more recent sins—sins of which you are now ashamed. It may have been an unkind word, a resentful attitude, or a lustful thought. Whatever it might be, God says He has put it out of His mind; He remembers it no more.

To remember no more is God's way of expressing absolute forgiveness. In Hebrews 8:12 (which quotes Jeremiah 31:34), God says, "For I will *forgive* their wickedness and will *remember* their sins *no more.*" And again in Hebrews 10:17-18, He says, "'Their sins and lawless acts I will *remember* no more.' And where these have been *forgiven,* there is no longer any sacrifice for sin" (emphasis added). Note that in both passages remembering no more is equated with forgiveness.

Psalm 130:3-4 states that same truth in a somewhat different way:

> If you, O LORD, kept a record of sins,
>   O Lord, who could stand?
> But with you there is forgiveness;
>   therefore you are feared.

Here the psalmist considers the prospect that God does remember our sins, that He does keep a record of them. If such were true, it would be a terrifying thought. The psalmist says, "Who could stand?" It is a rhetorical question. None of us could successfully stand before God's bar of judgment. But then the psalmist goes on to exclaim, "But with you there is forgiveness." God *does not* keep a record of our sins. Instead He forgives. This, of course, anticipates the sacrifice of Christ for our sins, for "without the shedding of blood there is no forgiveness" (Hebrews 9:22).

There is still another powerful metaphor in Micah 7:19, "You will . . . hurl all our iniquities into the depths of the sea." Notice the forceful verb, *hurl,* that Micah uses. The picture is of God vigorously disposing of our sins by hurling them overboard. He doesn't just drop them over the side or even pitch them overboard; He *hurls* them as something to be rid of and forgotten.

The picture here is of God eager to put away our sins. Because the sacrifice of His Son is of such infinite value, He delights to apply it to sinful men and women. God is not a reluctant forgiver; He is a joyous one. His justice having been satisfied and His wrath having been exhausted, He is now eager to extend His forgiveness to all who trust in His Son as their propitiatory sacrifice.

He hurls our sins overboard. What a picture of the way God treats our sins. Corrie ten Boom, a dear saint of the last century, used to say, "And then God put up a sign saying, 'No fishing allowed.'" Why would she say that? Because she knew that we tend to drag up our old sins, that we tend to live under a vague sense of guilt. She knew that we are not nearly as vigorous in appropriating God's forgiveness as He is in extending it. Consequently, instead of living in the sunshine of God's forgiveness through Christ, we tend to live under an overcast sky of guilt most of the time.

This is why God gave the Jews the picture of the scapegoat,

symbolically bearing away their sins. In addition to being a picture of what Jesus would do at the cross, it was an assurance to the Israelites that God had indeed honored the sacrifice of the slain goat and had put away their sins.

THE GREAT DAY OF ATONEMENT

Put yourself in the shoes of a devout Jew on the Day of Atonement. He sees the high priest slay the first goat as a propitiatory sacrifice. He watches as the priest disappears into the Tent of Meeting, knowing he is going into the Most Holy Place to sprinkle the blood of the slain goat on and before the mercy seat. He knows that only the high priest is allowed to enter that room (after ceremonial cleansing), and even then only once a year, and only with the blood of the sacrificial animal. Very conscious that atonement for his sins is conditioned on God's acceptance of the high priest's ministry, he waits with some degree of anxiety for the high priest to return.

Finally, after sprinkling the blood on the mercy seat, the high priest comes out and, in view of all the people, lays his hands on the live goat's head and confesses over it all the sins of the people. (In this act he symbolically transfers their sins to the goat.) All Israel hears his voice as he solemnly confesses, perhaps with weeping, all their wickedness and rebellion—all their sins. Then these devout Jews watch as the goat is led away into the desert bearing their sins.

Two things were necessary for the scapegoat ritual to be meaningful to an individual Jew. First, he must identify with the sins the high priest was confessing. He must acknowledge them as his own personal sins, not just the sins of the nation as a whole. Then he must by faith believe that the goat did indeed carry away those sins he acknowledged. He probably didn't understand how a goat could carry away his sins, but he believed that God had ordained this rite, and that somehow his sins had been removed from the presence of God and were no longer counted against him. His faith was not in the goat but in God, who had ordained the ritual of the goat.

So in order to subjectively benefit from the work of the high priest on the Day of Atonement, the individual Israelite had to exercise both penitence and faith. Penitence is a sincere and humble acknowledgment of one's sins. Faith, in this instance, is believing God's testimony that his sins were transferred to the goat and that the guilt of them no longer hung over his head.

Of course the scapegoat could not itself carry away the sins of the people. It was only symbolic—a *type* of the true scapegoat who was to come, Jesus Christ. Today we see the reality of the symbol. We see Jesus as the One who not only propitiated the wrath of God, symbolized by the sacrifice of the first goat, but who also removed our sins from the presence of God, symbolized by the second goat led away into the desert, bearing the sins of the people.

The same two attitudes, penitence and faith, are necessary for all of us today who trust in Jesus as our scapegoat. In coming to Christ for salvation we must acknowledge ourselves as sinners before a holy God. We must, so to speak, lay our hands on Christ's head and confess over Him all our transgression and rebellion. This does not mean we confess every single individual sin. It does mean that we acknowledge ourselves as sinners before a holy God and that we face up to particular sins we are aware of.

But it is not just in coming to Christ that we must exercise penitence and faith. Rather, these two heartfelt attitudes should characterize our lives throughout every day. We not only come to God through faith in Christ as both our propitiation and our scapegoat, we must live in His presence every day on the same basis.

Objectively, our sins have been put away. To use the language of the Scriptures we have been looking at, they are completely removed, put behind God's back, blotted out, remembered no more, and hurled into the depths of the sea. Subjectively, however, we must *believe* the testimony of God that they truly have been put away. We must believe that, just as the Old Testament scapegoat symbolically carried away the sins of the Jews from the presence of God, so Jesus actually carried away our sins.

CLEANSING OUR CONSCIENCES

God has given each of us a conscience, a moral compass within our hearts, bearing witness to His Law. In sinful or self-righteous people (that is, people whose dominant characteristics are either obvious sin or obvious self-righteousness) the conscience is to some degree "hardened." That is, it is relatively insensitive to sin or its own self-righteousness. But in a growing Christian the conscience becomes more and more sensitive to violations of God's Law. As a result, our consciences continually indict us, accusing us of not only particular sins, but, more important, of our overall sinfulness. We recognize more and more that specific acts of sin are simply the expressions of our still-wicked hearts. Our sinfulness is very real to us, and we find it difficult to believe that God would no longer remember each offense.

It is here that we must by faith see Jesus bearing our sin and carrying it away forever from the presence of God. I find it helpful to visualize the Old Testament scapegoat carrying away the sins of the people that have been laid on its head, and then remind myself that this is an accurate picture of what Jesus did with my sin. In fact, Christ's work on my behalf is greater still.

When contrasting the Old Testament types with the reality in Christ that they prefigured, the writer of Hebrews uses the phrase *how much more.* He writes, "How much more, then, will the blood of Christ, who through the eternal Spirit offered himself unblemished to God, cleanse our consciences from acts that lead to death, so that we may serve the living God" (Hebrews 9:14). It is only the blood of Christ that can cleanse our consciences and quiet their accusations against us. But to experience this cleansing subjectively we must agree with our consciences in a true attitude of penitence, and then by faith appropriate the reality of that cleansing blood. This does not mean *our* knowledge of sin is taken away, but that the growing burden of uncanceled guilt ceases.

In Romans 4:8 Paul writes, "Blessed is the man whose sin the Lord will never count against him." Do you believe that the sin you are so painfully and shamefully aware of now will never be counted against you? If by faith you see Jesus as your scapegoat, you will subjectively experience the reality of that wonderful truth. Then, in the words of Hebrews 9:14, you will be freed from a guilty conscience so that you may serve the living God.

EXPIATION

Now that we have looked at the beautiful imagery of the scapegoat and have seen how that symbol pictures the reality of Christ removing our sin from the presence of God and from our own consciences, let me introduce you to another seldom-used and little-understood theological word: *expiation*. You can readily see its spelling similarity to *propitiation*. In fact, the two words are often confused, but they are significantly different in meaning.

Propitiation, as we saw in chapter 5, addresses the wrath of God. It is the work of Christ saving us from God's wrath by absorbing it in His own person as our substitute. *Expiation*, which basically means "removal," accompanies propitiation and speaks of the work of Christ in removing or putting away our sin. Such is the symbolism of the two goats used on the Day of Atonement. The first goat represented Christ's work of *propitiation* as it was killed and its blood sprinkled on the mercy seat. The second goat represented Christ's work of *expiation* in removing or blotting out the sins that were against us. The object of propitiation is the wrath of God. The object of expiation is the sin, which must be removed from His presence.

Because of the reluctance of some scholars to accept the idea of the wrath of God, they have replaced propitiation with expiation. They have, in effect, eliminated the first goat of the Day of Atonement. But the two goats together constituted one offering, and both goats represented the work of Christ on our behalf. It would have been a blasphemous affront to a holy God to send one goat away into the desert without first sacrificing the goat whose blood symbolized the blood of Christ that alone propitiates the wrath of God.

It is not necessary in your Christian growth that you make *expiation* a part of your vocabulary, but it is necessary that you make the *concept* of sin's removal, symbolized by the scapegoat, a part of your thinking and theology. Only then, as we saw in Hebrews 9:14, will you be freed from your guilt so that you can serve God effectively.

Do you grasp in both your heart and mind what the message of the scapegoat says to you? Do you believe that Jesus really has carried away your sin and that God has indeed removed it as far as the east is from the west? Do you by faith lay hold of the glorious truth that God has put all your sin behind His back, that He has blotted it from His record and remembers it no more? Do you rejoice in the fact that God has hurled your sin into the depths of the sea and will never count it against you? Do you see God showing us in all these wonderful Old Testament metaphors that the work of Christ is infinitely greater than the greatest depth of your sin?

The work of Christ is finished. Nothing more remains to be done. God's wrath has been propitiated. Our sins have been removed. The question is, will we appreciate it, not only at our initial moment of salvation, but for our day-to-day acceptance with God? It is only as we do the latter that we will truly begin to appreciate the glory of the cross and the unsearchable riches of Christ.

CHAPTER SEVEN

RANSOMED!

———

On the night of March 1, 1932, the eighteen-month-old son of famous aviator Charles Lindbergh was kidnapped from his nursery by a man who used a ladder to climb to the second-story room. The kidnapper left a crudely written note on the windowsill demanding a ransom of $50,000 in $20, $10, and $5 bills. Because of Lindbergh's fame as the first person to fly nonstop across the Atlantic just five years before, the story made headlines in nearly every newspaper across the country.

Despite the ransom demand, the kidnapper had actually murdered the child the same night. The body was found seventy-two days afterward in the woods near the Lindberghs' home. Two and a half years after the kidnapping a carpenter was arrested after passing one of the ransom bills at a service station. Despite his denial of guilt, the man was convicted of first-degree murder and eventually executed in the electric chair.

Kidnapping and *ransom* are words we usually associate together, though obviously they are not part of our everyday vocabulary. But when we do hear of a kidnapping, we immediately wonder what ransom has been demanded.

The word *ransom* has not always been associated primarily with kidnapping. Centuries ago, it was the payment given to an enemy country to secure the release of prisoners of war, particularly important prisoners. In Bible times a ransom was the price paid to gain freedom for a slave. To pay a ransom was to purchase back someone who was being held in captivity or slavery.

How then are we to understand the words of Jesus that "the Son of Man did not come to be served, but to serve, and to give his life as a *ransom* for many" (Matthew 20:28, emphasis added)? We cannot fully answer this question without examining the biblical use of a related word, *redeem*. To *redeem* is to buy back or secure the release of someone from slavery or from captivity by the payment of a ransom. Redemption, then, is the action to secure release; the *ransom* is the price paid to effect the action. It is also true, however, that *ransom* may be used as a verb, meaning the same thing as *to redeem*.

Jesus said He would give His life as a ransom for many (see Mark 10:45). Clearly His life was considered as a ransom payment. Just what was the captivity from which the "many" are ransomed? Hebrews 9:15 tells us that Jesus "died as a ransom to set them free from the sins committed under the first covenant." But again, what does it mean to be set free from sins committed under the first covenant?

The apostle Paul answered the question in Galatians 3:13: "Christ redeemed us from the curse of the law by becoming a curse for us." To be set free from the sins committed under the first covenant and to be redeemed from the curse of the Law are essentially synonymous expressions. Christ shed His blood and gave His life as a ransom to redeem us from this curse. As a captive held in chains is set free when the ransom is paid, so all who trust in Christ are set free from the condemnation and curse of the Law.

UNDER A CURSE

Why was it necessary for Christ to give His life as a ransom to redeem us from the curse of the Law? Why are we under a curse from which we need to be redeemed? In Galatians 3:10 Paul wrote, "All who rely on observing the law are under a curse, for it is written: 'Cursed is everyone who does not continue to do everything written in the Book of the Law.'" Mankind was under a curse because we had not perfectly obeyed the Law of God — either in Adam or as individuals.

The curse falls on everyone who does not continue to do *everything* written in the Book of the Law. This is an impossibly exacting standard. At the U.S. Air Force Academy near my home, the minimum requirement for graduation is a C average (commonly known as a 2.0 grade point average (GPA) on a maximum scale of 4.0). Civilian institutions may vary in their requirements, but no university or college demands a perfect 4.0 GPA for graduation. If they did, only a scant few would graduate. But Paul tells us this is what the Law of God demands. The old Ivory soap slogan, "99 44/100 percent pure" apparently denotes quite an accomplishment in the manufacture of soap, but such a percentage is not good enough to satisfy the Law of God. Rather it pronounces a curse on the least failure to do *everything* written in it.

What are the effects of the curse? According to George Smeaton, "It consisted especially in the privation of God, . . . for the wors[t] ingredient of the curse is the loss of God, or the absence and complete withdrawal of God from a human soul, made to be His habitation."[1] I'm sure we cannot comprehend what the loss of God means, and in fact, many people today think they would be happy to get rid of Him. But we need to remember that as Jesus hung on the cross bearing the curse in our place and experiencing unimaginable agony, His only cry of anguish was, "My God, my God, why have you forsaken me?"(Matthew 27:46).

For a faint idea of the curse of the Law, look at God's promised blessings and threatened curses to the nation of Israel recorded in Deuteronomy 28. In that chapter Moses set forth blessings for obedience (verses 1-14) and curses for disobedience (verses 15-68). The promised blessings were "out of this world," to use a modern superlative. By contrast, the threatened curses were horrible beyond anything we can imagine. For example, one aspect of the curse would be a siege so severe that genteel women would be driven to cannibalize their own children.

Read through Deuteronomy 28 slowly, allowing the full impact of the threatened curses to sink in. Keep in mind that the promised blessings and threatened curses were only temporal in nature, having to do with the nation of Israel in the Promised Land. Then consider that the extreme severity of the threatened curses only begin to picture the unimaginable agony of being under the curse of God for all eternity.

Some may react strongly to the rigorous demand of the Law for absolutely perfect obedience and the severity of the curse for its least infraction. Why is 99 44/100 percent not good enough? Why does God insist on 100 percent obedience? After all, we may reason, even highway patrolmen usually allow a five- to ten-mile-per-hour violation of the speed limit before ticketing us.

Yet even in ordinary life, in many instances there is no room for the least deviation from the law or the rules of a game. Officials in a football game do not allow for "just a little bit" of being off-sides. Rather, the least infraction is penalized. Or consider a bank.

How could it tolerate "just a little bit" of embezzlement by each of its tellers?

Above all, when we think that the Law of God is too rigorous or its curse too severe, it is because we don't understand God or the nature of sin. God is transcendent in His majesty and sovereign in His authority. Every sin, be it ever so small in our eyes, is an assault on that authority. In effect we are saying, "I don't care what *You* say. I will do as *I* please this time." Furthermore, God has commanded us to be holy as He is holy. Therefore, each sin is an insult to His character. It's as if we are saying to God, "I don't want to be like You." Think what a rebellious affront it would be for a child to say that to his parent.

In the final analysis, however, we should not try to justify God for the exactness of His Law or the severity of its sanctions. After all, God is God; He is the Creator. He is the One who brought the whole universe into existence by His spoken command. He is the One on whom each of us depends for life and breath. He is the One who has the absolute right to establish the rules of the game, the laws by which we are to live. And He is the One who has the right to attach sanctions to those laws for breaking them.

REDEMPTION FROM THE CURSE

The primary purpose of the Law, however, is not to curse us but to lead us to Christ (see Galatians 3:24). God does not take pleasure in the death of the wicked (see Ezekiel 18:23). Rather, as Paul wrote in Galatians 3:13, "Christ redeemed us from the curse of the law by becoming a curse for us." The language is emphatic; Christ became a curse, which means He became a curse-bearer. George Smeaton notes that the use of the word *curse* as a noun (as in curse-bearer) rather than as an adjective indicates the highest conceivable measure or degree.[2] So when Jesus emptied the cup of God's wrath, He endured the ultimate limit of the Law's curse.

Christ became a curse for us. Literally, He became a curse in our place as our substitute. He experienced the full fury of the curse that we should have experienced. It is true He did it *for* us, but He did it for us by doing it *in our place* as our appointed substitute.

Once again we see the importance of our legal union with Christ, which I first introduced in chapter 3. Because He was our God-appointed legal representative, He was legally qualified to endure the curse in our place as our substitute. There is no adequate analogy for this union in human experience. One person may pay a financial debt, such as a traffic fine, for someone else, but no one can serve a prison sentence as a substitute for another. In human jurisprudence, a moral debt such as a prison sentence can only be served by the person who has incurred the debt.

Many people who deny the substitutionary nature of Christ's atonement claim that it is unjust for an innocent person to suffer in place of the guilty. That is true in a human legal system, but again we must remember that it is God who established the curse for breaking His Law, and it is God who ordained the remedy for the curse. Human analogies and principles by which we operate are often helpful in illustrating the truths of Scripture, but they should never be used to refute Scripture.

Above all, however, we should accept this wonderful truth that Jesus bore the curse in our place and paid our ransom price, not because it seems reasonable by any human standards, but because God in His Word has declared it to be so.

Knowing that Christ paid our ransom price, you might now wonder to whom the ransom was paid. Some have thought the ransom was paid to Satan, who holds unbelievers captive (see, for example, Acts 26:18; Colossians 1:13; 2 Timothy 2:26). This cannot possibly be true. If it were, there would be a sense in which Satan was victorious over Christ. If we were to think of the ransom price in terms of money, Satan would be "laughing all the way to the bank." The obvious answer to the question is that the ransom was paid to God acting in His capacity as Judge. It was God's justice that Jesus satisfied. It was His cup of wrath that Jesus emptied. And it was His curse that Jesus bore as He paid our ransom price.

Once again we see that human analogies of biblical truths ultimately break down when pressed to every detail. In human experience a ransom is paid to an enemy or adversary; the kidnapper, the army that has captured prisoners of war, or the slaveholder. But God both demanded the ransom price and paid it in the death of His Son. Again, in human experience we recognize the distinction between the ransom—that is, the price paid—and the redeemer, the one who pays the price. Jesus, however, was both the redeemer and the ransom as He laid down His life in our place.

We should never cease to be amazed that the One who established the Law and determined its curse should Himself ransom us from that curse by bearing it in our place. As George Smeaton wrote,

> The ransom which liberated us was not his divine doctrine, nor his bright example of holiness left us to follow. . . . The apostle [Paul] thinks of the ransom in a far other way: he identifies it with the Lord's abasement and ignominious death as a vicarious satisfaction. He

affirms that the price by which He discharged us from temporal and eternal penalty was his being made a curse for us by entering into our position before God.[3]

O, what wondrous love; O, what infinite wisdom! Our glorious God devised such a plan that satisfies His justice and upholds His Law while at the same time providing a complete redemption for us from the curse of His Law. Surely we need to say often the words of Jonah when he cried out from the belly of the fish, "Salvation comes from the LORD" (Jonah 2:9).

BLESSINGS OF REDEMPTION

There is still more good news. In Galatians 4:4-5 Paul wrote, "God sent his Son, born of a woman, born under law, to redeem those under law, that we might receive the full rights of sons." By redeeming us from the curse of the Law, Jesus opened the way for us to inherit the blessing of obedience to it, blessings that He earned for us by His own perfect obedience.

Here the blessing is identified as "the full rights of sons." The reference is to the status of sons who have advanced from their minority to that of full-grown young adults. Thus we have been redeemed from a cell on death row and have been brought into God's family as fully adopted sons, with all the privileges included in that status. Think of what this would mean on a human level. Here sits a man on death row, convicted of heinous crimes. He is in solitary confinement twenty-three hours a day. All legal appeals to spare him have been exhausted, and his impending execution looms nearer every day.

Suddenly the cell door is flung open, and the judge who sentenced him stands there with a full pardon in his hand. But he carries more than a mere pardon. He also carries papers of adoption into his own family. The judge who sentenced this man to die has now adopted him as his own son. This death-row inmate is not just put out on the street with a cheap suit of clothes and a hundred dollars. No, he is taken into the home of the judge himself and provided with all the love and care the judge lavishes on his own children.

But the good news keeps getting better. We truly did live on God's eternal "death row." As Paul wrote in Romans 6:23, "the wages of sin is death"—physical *and* eternal death. That's where we were—on death row. As believers we know that we have been delivered from eternal death, but we still face the prospect of physical death. That is not the final word, however. In the same letter Paul wrote that "we wait eagerly for our adoption as sons, the *redemption* of our bodies" (Romans 8:23, emphasis added). This means our redemption from the curse of the Law and adoption into God's family will reach its ultimate fulfillment at the Resurrection, when we receive our immortal bodies and dwell forever in the immediate presence of the Lord. We will explore these blessings in greater detail in chapter 14, but we must consider one more issue now.

REDEMPTION FROM OUR FORMER WAY OF LIFE

Let's pursue the story of the death-row criminal who is not only pardoned but adopted into the judge's family. Would you want to be a member of that family as they welcomed this murderer into their home? Suppose he had been convicted as a serial killer who bludgeoned his victims to death. Would you sleep peacefully in your bed at night, or would you want to lock and bar your door before going to bed? Regardless of the change in the man's legal status, we obviously would be apprehensive, wondering if we might be his next victim. We would all agree that this man needs not only a change of legal status but also a change of heart. We don't want to sleep in the same house with a serial killer.

Once again we reach the limitations of human illustrations. The judge who brings the pardon and who adopts this murderer into his family cannot change this man's heart. But God *can* and *does* change our hearts. God promises to take away our hearts of stone that are spiritually dead and unresponsive to Him and give us hearts of flesh that are spiritually alive and responsive to Him (see Ezekiel 36:26). God changes not only our legal status, but our hearts as well. To go back to the illustration, we no longer have the heart of a serial killer. This, too, is part of our redemption that Jesus secured for us.

In the story of redemption, deliverance from the penal curse of the Law is the major part of the story, but it is not the whole story. The apostle Peter wrote that "you were redeemed from the empty way of life handed down to you from your forefathers" (1 Peter 1:18). The empty way of life is the life we lived without Christ. Regardless of whether it was a decent life or a wicked life judged on a human scale of morality, it was a vain, futile, empty life. A good description of this empty life is found in Ephesians 2:2-3, where Paul describes us as having followed the ways of the world and of Satan, and of having continually gratified the cravings of our sinful natures. Christ's ransom, then, secured for us not only redemption from the penal curse of the Law, but also redemption from this bondage to sin. *These two aspects of redemption always go together.* Redemption from the curse infallibly secures redemption from the bondage.

The apostle Paul addressed this absolute connection between redemption from the curse of the Law and redemption from the bondage of sin when he wrote that Jesus Christ "gave himself for us *to redeem us from all wickedness* and to purify for himself a people that are his very own, eager to do what is good" (Titus 2:14, emphasis added). Here we see that the design of Christ's redemptive work goes beyond salvation from God's everlasting curse. Its purpose is to redeem us *from* sin *to* Himself to be a people who desire to please Him.

Regarding this absolute connection between redemption from the guilt and consequent curse of sin and the release from the dominion or reign of sin in our lives, noted New Testament scholar Leon Morris wrote, "It is wrong to separate the legal status, gained by complete discharge of the law against us, from the resultant life. The only redemption Paul knew was one in which they lived as those who had been adopted into the family of God."[4]

A Daily Response

We have now seen yet another aspect of the unsearchable riches of Christ. We have been ransomed from death row, adopted into the Father's family, and given new hearts so that our major bent is to live for Him. All this is set against the dark background of the curse of the Law for *any* disobedience, which of course affects us all. Just as the diamonds on a jeweler's counter shine more brilliantly when set upon a dark velvet pad, so Christ's redemptive work shines more brilliantly when contrasted with our sin and the consequent curse that was upon us.

The fact is, however, that even as believers we continue to

sin even though we are no longer under its dominion. And when we sin—and even our best deeds are stained with sin— we do that which apart from Christ would call down God's curse upon us. Our consciences know that and will continually bring accusations against us. Our only safe response is to plead guilty to those accusations without trying to minimize them. Having done that, we must go back to the gospel and remind ourselves that the curse of the Law no longer has a claim against us. And then in grateful response to what God has done for us in Christ, we set ourselves to put to death by the power of the Spirit those very sins of which our consciences condemn us. Only in this way can we continually glory in the cross and enjoy the unsearchable riches of Christ.

RECONCILIATION

Justin Carter was seething. He'd just been grounded from driving the family car—not for a week, nor even for a month, but indefinitely. Justin was only a few weeks past his sixteenth birthday—the day he'd finally gotten his drivers' license. Now he'd been ticketed for speeding—fifty miles per hour in a thirty-miles-per-hour zone. He wasn't too concerned about the four penalty points against his drivers' license or the hefty fine he'd had to pay. In a sense, that was a badge of honor, a rite of passage in the crowd he was running with.

What really got to Justin was losing the privilege of driving the family car. What would his friends think? Instead of being cool, now he'd be laughed at. Even worse, his best friend, Tony, had been with him when his mom and dad made their pronouncement: no more driving their car until he changed his rebellious attitude.

Justin's pleading soon escalated to ranting and raving, then to outright belligerence. This wasn't the first conflict he'd had with his parents. In fact, his rebellious attitude had been growing steadily since he'd made some new friends at school two years ago. His parents had firmly and consistently tried to rein him in—to no avail. But this was the last straw for Justin—he wasn't going to take it anymore.

"I'm getting outta here," he announced defiantly to his parents. "I'm gonna go live with Tony. His parents aren't old-fashioned and strict like you. They let Tony do whatever he wants. I'm gonna go have a life."

With that Justin stomped off to his room, where he hastily threw some clothes into his duffel bag. Returning back through the living room, he gave his parents not so much as a glance, nor a word of good-bye. He slammed the front door and headed for Tony's car at the curb.

Justin got more than he bargained for at Tony's house. For one thing, Tony was always bickering with his two younger brothers. Worse yet, the parents constantly yelled at the boys and at each other. One night Tony's dad came home drunk and began to curse at and threaten them. Justin was shaken. He'd never been cursed at before. Still, he couldn't go home. He had defied his parents and he couldn't back down. He had too much pride.

Tony's mother never cooked for them. She'd send out for pizza or pick up something at the supermarket deli. At first this was great. No more "eat your vegetables" edicts like Justin had grown up with. But after a while it started to grow old. He began to remember Mom's good cooking, something he'd always taken for granted. He could almost taste her meatloaf.

Justin started to think more and more of home. He remembered how his dad had always been there for him. He thought of his mother's care and how she'd driven him to so many soccer games—a sport he'd really loved until he began to run with that new crowd.

Slowly Justin began to come to his senses. He realized the total freedom Tony had wasn't a mark of his parents' love, but rather of their indifference. With that came the realization that his own parents' attempts to deal with his rebellion were a demonstration of their love for him. Maybe being a bit old-fashioned wasn't so bad. After all, *his* dad never came home drunk. Justin's mind was made up. He'd call Mom right now.

"Mom," Justin began slowly, "I want to come back home." It was a request, not an announcement. He knew very well what a pain he'd been to his parents the last couple of years, and he wasn't sure what response he'd get.

"You do?" his mom responded with a slight hesitation in her voice. She had no idea what to expect if Justin returned. Would it be more of the same rebellious spirit? Would he continue trying to take advantage of them? Would the same old tensions flare up?

Justin's heart sank as he detected her hesitancy. What if they wouldn't take him back? What would he do? He was sick of Tony's house. "Yeah, I do, Mom. I really do." Now there was just a hint of pleading in his voice. He really did want to go home.

The mother's heart went out to her son. She sensed the pleading in his voice. "Why don't you come on home, and when your dad gets home we'll talk about it."

"Okay, Mom, I'll be there by six," Justin said with hope in his voice. But as he hung up the phone, he wasn't as hopeful. Had he forever ruined his relationship with his parents?

Justin waited to return until his father came home from work. He wanted to talk to both Mom and Dad together. Furthermore, he asked Tony to drive him home and to come in while he talked to them. He had rehearsed what he would say, and he wanted Tony to hear it.

"Mom and Dad," he said, "I'm sorry for the way I've treated you the last two years. I've been a real jerk, but I've come to realize you attempted to deal with my rebellion not because you're old-fashioned, but because you love me. Now I want to change. I want my life to be like it was before. I want to be the obedient and happy son I used to be. Will you forgive me and take me back?"

Justin was thoroughly chastened and repentant.

"And Mom and Dad," he continued, "I was belligerent toward you in front of Tony, so I asked him to come in to hear what I've said to you. He heard me defy you, so it's only right that he should hear me ask your forgiveness." And then turning to Tony, he said, "Will you also forgive me for mistreating my parents in your presence?"

Tony was taken aback. Never in his entire life had he heard anyone ask forgiveness of someone else. He didn't know what to make of it. He just stammered, "Sure, man" and then said, "I'd better get going." With that he beat a hasty retreat out the front door.

Justin's mother and father moved quickly to embrace Justin and assure him of their forgiveness. After dinner, they settled down in the living room, where Justin shared the lessons he'd learned and the changes he wanted to make. His parents were obviously thrilled and promised to help Justin regain the kind of life he'd lived before.

That night Justin was *reconciled* to his parents.

RECONCILIATION TO GOD

The story of Justin Carter's reconciliation with his parents illustrates to some degree our reconciliation to God. Reconciliation, by definition, assumes a previous state of alienation and hostility caused by the offensive actions of one or both parties. In Justin's case, the alienation from his parents was due entirely to his own sinful rebellion. Though he blamed his parents, the estrangement was solely his fault.

In this sense Justin represents us all. It is our sin that has separated us from God (see Isaiah 59:2). It is our sinful state that has caused us to be "God's enemies" (Romans 5:10) — that is, those hated by God. "Those hated by God?" you ask. Does God actually hate people? Yes, the psalmist wrote, "You hate all who do wrong" (Psalm 5:5). So when Paul described us as God's enemies, he was not at that point describing our sinful hatred of God, but rather His righteous hatred of us because of our sin.

Because of the sinful connotations we always associate with human hatred, it is difficult for us to conceive of God's holy hatred toward people. But God's hatred is simply His just and holy revulsion against sin and His holy antagonism toward those who rebel against Him.

It is for this reason that God's act of reconciling us to Himself through the death of Christ is so amazing. Justin's reconciliation to his parents was due to his change of heart, his attitude of repentance, and his actions of acknowledging his sin and asking their forgiveness. But in our case we were powerless to do anything (see Romans 5:6). We could not help ourselves; nor would we even want to do so, left to ourselves. As Paul wrote in Romans 8:7, "The sinful mind is hostile to God." In our natural state, not one of us would want to be reconciled to God.

The good news of the gospel, though, is that God Himself took the initiative by sending His Son to die in our place to satisfy His justice and absorb His wrath. Justin Carter's parents did not—and, in their situation, could not—make the first move. There could be no reconciliation until Justin had a change of heart. But God did not wait for a change of heart on our part. He made the first move. Indeed, He did more than that. He did *all* that was necessary to secure our reconciliation, including our change of heart. Even though He is the One offended by our sin, He is the One who makes amends to Himself through the death of Christ. As Paul wrote in 2 Corinthians 5:19, "God was reconciling the world to himself in Christ, not counting men's sins against them."

In Justin's story, his confession and repentance might seem a bit overstated. In real life, would a sixteen-year-old boy humble himself before one of his friends as Justin did? Would he ask forgiveness for mistreating his parents in his friend's presence? Probably not. But a total reconciliation demands a total effort by the offending party to make amends. This is what Justin did, and this is the only way in which his actions can, in a limited sense, picture our Lord's work of reconciliation. Justin did all that was required to be fully reconciled to his parents. There were no smoldering issues left unaddressed. His parents were completely satisfied, and thus he was completely restored to their favor.

When Jesus satisfied the justice of God and propitiated the wrath of God, He did all that was required to remove the enmity of God toward us. By His death He bridged the vast gulf of divine alienation between us and objectively restored us to a position of friendship and favor with God. But again we must keep in mind that it was God, the offended party, who sent His Son to reconcile us to Himself. As Paul wrote in Romans 5:10, "When we were God's enemies, we were reconciled to him through the death of his Son."

Of course, this historical, objective work of reconciliation by Christ has to be personally received by each of us. That is why Paul wrote in 2 Corinthians 5:19-20, "And he [God] has committed to us the message of reconciliation. We are therefore Christ's ambassadors, as though God were making his appeal through us. We implore you on Christ's behalf: Be reconciled to God."

This is a most amazing passage of Scripture. Having objectively secured reconciliation for us, Christ now appeals to us through His gospel messengers to "be reconciled to God" — that is, to receive His work of reconciliation. Think about what that means. We ourselves should have been on our faces before

God, imploring Him to be reconciled to us. Instead, we see God reconciling us to Himself through the death of His Son, and then appealing to us to receive that reconciliation. What a pure act of grace and mercy on God's part!

To add to our amazement, we know that, left to ourselves, we would never even *want* to be reconciled to God. According to Paul, we were so blinded by Satan that we could not even see the light of the gospel and receive it (see 2 Corinthians 4:4). Therefore God sends His Holy Spirit to open our hearts to understand and receive the message of reconciliation (see Acts 16:14). O, what wondrous love, what matchless grace, that God would do everything necessary to reconcile us to Himself.

A PERMANENT CHANGE

There is one more significant difference between Justin Carter's reconciliation with his parents and our reconciliation to God. There would always be the possibility that Justin might at some time revert to his former rebellious state. In that case he would again be alienated from his parents. It would be a self-inflicted alienation, to be sure, but nevertheless a real one. In fact, his parents' displeasure might even be stronger the second time around.

Happily for us, however, our reconciliation to God is permanent and eternal. Because Christ accomplished it for us, there is no possibility it can ever be undone. Though we continue, even as believers, to do those things that in themselves deserve God's displeasure, we can never revert to a state of divine alienation. For the sake of Christ, God will always accept us. And even when God deems it necessary to discipline us for persistent disobedience, He always does so out of love to restore us to the way of obedience (see Hebrews 12:4-11).

We will see in chapter 15 that this reconciliation does—in fact, it must—affect the way we live. The very nature of our salvation guarantees that we will not continue in an absolute state of sin and rebellion against God. He not only saves us from sin's guilt and consequent alienation, He also delivers us from sin's reign and continues to work to progressively free us from sin's activity in our lives. However, in the midst of God's work and our struggle with indwelling sin, we must always keep in mind that our status of favor and friendship with God is always, and ever will be, based on the objective work of Christ for us as our representative and substitute. We have been forever reconciled to God through the death of His Son.

LOOKING BACK

We have now looked at Christ's work for us from six different points of view. We have seen that He:

- Perfectly obeyed the Law of God
- Satisfied the justice of God
- Exhausted the wrath of God
- Removed our sins from the presence of God
- Redeemed us from the curse of God
- Reconciled us to God

One thing is readily apparent: Every work of Christ is directed toward God. It is His Law that was obeyed, His justice that was satisfied, His wrath that was propitiated, His holy presence from which our sins were removed, His curse from which we were redeemed, and alienation from His divine presence that has been reconciled.

This Godward focus of Christ's atoning work tells us that it is the integrity of God's moral government and the upholding of His honor and glory that is the primary issue in our salvation. It is true that it is the love of God for sinful people such as you and me that is the wellspring of our salvation, but it is also true that this love could only be shown in such a way that the glory of His holiness and the honor of His Law would be magnified. And Jesus in His sinless life and sin-bearing death did just that. Hallelujah, what a Savior!

As we contemplate the glory of the cross, then, we must see that not only is our deepest need of salvation met, but that it has been done in such a way as to bring the most glory to God Himself. It is at the cross where God's Law and God's grace are both most brilliantly displayed, where His justice and His mercy are both glorified. But it is also at the cross where we are most humbled. It is at the cross where we admit to God and to ourselves that there is absolutely nothing we can do to earn or merit our salvation. As someone has said so well, "We bring nothing to our salvation except our sin that made it necessary."

When we are gripped by these truths in the very core of our being, then we will begin to gaze with amazement at the unsearchable riches of Christ. Then we will gladly say with Paul, "God forbid that I should glory, save in the cross of our Lord Jesus Christ" (Galatians 6:14, KJV).

CHAPTER NINE

RIGHT STANDING WITH GOD

In his best-selling book *When Bad Things Happen to Good People*, Rabbi Harold Kushner wrote,

> "There is only one question which really matters: why do bad things happen to good people? All other theological conversation is intellectually diverting; somewhat like doing crossword puzzles in the Sunday paper and feeling very satisfied when you have made the words fit; but ultimately without the capacity to reach people where they really care."[1]

Rabbi Kushner wrote that book as a result of the tragic life and death of his firstborn son, who died at the age of fourteen from a rare disease called *progeria*, or "rapid aging." I once saw Rabbi Kushner on television, and he came across as a kind and gentle man, the type of person you would be glad to have as your next-door neighbor. And as a father and grandfather, I appreciate the emotional anguish out of which he wrote. Having said that, however, I must respectfully but profoundly disagree with his conclusion as to the only question that really matters.

Setting aside the issue of whether there is *only one* question that really matters, the Bible would say to us that, in light of eternity, the *most important* question we all face is: How can a sinful man or woman come into a right relationship with an infinitely holy and just God? After all, Jesus said, "What good is it for a man to gain the whole world, yet forfeit his soul?" (Mark 8:36). Suppose a person lives his entire life experiencing nothing but prosperity and happiness, yet dies without a right relationship with God. What has he gained? Actually, he has lost everything.

What then does it mean to have a right relationship with God? Because God Himself is perfectly righteous and cannot look with favor on any unrighteousness, the only way we can have a right relationship with Him is to be perfectly righteous—as He is righteous. But that's our problem, for, as Paul wrote, "There is no one righteous, not even one" (Romans 3:10). What are we to do? Should we try harder? That will not help us, because, as Paul observed, "Therefore no one will be declared righteous in [God's] sight by observing the law; rather, through the law we become conscious of sin" (Romans 3:20). Regardless of how hard we try, we will never attain the perfect righteousness that God will accept. So the question remains: How may we attain a right relationship with God?

THE RIGHTEOUSNESS OF GOD

Happily, the apostle Paul answers this question in Romans 3:21-26. After describing our predicament in verse 20, Paul announces that God has provided a solution for us: "A righteousness from God, apart from law, has been made known" (verse 21).

What is this righteousness from God—or, more literally stated, the righteousness *of* God? In the famous story of Martin Luther's life, Luther at first thought the righteousness of God was the righteousness that God required of us in perfectly fulfilling His Law. Because he realized more and more he could not possibly measure up to that impossible demand, he grew increasingly angry with God. At one time he had exclaimed, "Love God? I hate him."[2] Eventually he came to realize that the righteousness of God was that which God provided for us. At that time he said, "Thereupon I felt myself reborn and to have gone through open doors into paradise."[3]

What then is this righteousness from God that Paul announces to us, and over which Martin Luther struggled? *It is a righteousness that He both requires and provides for us.* It is the righteousness that He requires because it must fully satisfy the utmost demands of His Law, both in its precepts and penalty. For although this righteousness is apart from Law as far as we are concerned, it is not as far as God is concerned. Rather it must be a righteousness that both perfectly fulfills the righteous requirements of His Law and satisfies the demands of His justice toward those who have broken His Law.

This righteousness from God, then, is nothing less than the perfect righteousness of Jesus Christ, who, through His sinless life and His death in obedience to the Father's will, perfectly fulfilled the Law of God in both its precepts and its penalty. In other words, this righteousness that God both requires and provides embraces all the work of Christ that we have been studying up to this point.

JUSTIFICATION

This leads us to a biblical word that is one of Paul's major themes in both Romans and Galatians: *justification*. The word occurs (usually as the verb *justify*) about forty times in the

New Testament, mostly in Paul's writings. A helpful approach to understanding its meaning is to look again at Romans 3:20, where Paul wrote that "no one will be *declared righteous* in his sight by observing the law" (emphasis added). A literal translation is, "No one will be *justified* in his sight by works of the law." To *justify*, then, is to declare righteous. *Justification* is God's declaration that we are righteous before Him.

For us, justification means that God has forgiven all our sins and accepts us as righteous in His sight. How can this be? How can God accept us as righteous when our very best deeds fall so far short of the righteous demands of His Law? The answer lies in our federal or legal union with Christ.

We considered our legal union with Christ in chapter 3, but it will be helpful to review it at this point. In all of human history God has appointed two men to act as the federal heads, or legal representatives, of two groups of people. Adam was appointed by God to represent the entire human race, with the exception of Jesus. Because of our representative union with him, when he sinned, we sinned. I've addressed this issue more fully in chapter 2.

Jesus was appointed to be a federal head to represent in both His life and death all who will ever trust in Him. This is why Paul makes such statements as, "I have been crucified with Christ" (Galatians 2:20), and, "Now if we died with Christ, we believe that we will also live with him" (Romans 6:8). We were crucified with Christ or died with Him because He was our representative in both His life and death. Because we are united by faith to Him who is perfectly righteous, God accepts us as perfectly righteous. God does not resort to some kind of legal fiction, calling something righteous that is not. Rather, He declares us righteous on the basis of the real accomplished righteousness of Christ, imputed to us because of our union with Him.

The apostle Paul expressed it very succinctly in my favorite verse of Scripture, 2 Corinthians 5:21: "God made him who had no sin to be sin for us, so that in him [through union with him] we might become the righteousness of God." That is, God took our sin and imputed (charged) it to Christ, and took His righteousness and imputed (credited) it to us. To put it in a very contemporary form, God treated Christ as we deserved to be treated, so that He might treat us as Christ deserved to be treated.

THE ROLE AND NATURE OF FAITH

Returning to Romans 3:21-26, we read in verse 22, "This righteousness from God comes through faith in Jesus Christ to all who believe." It is through faith in Christ, then, that we experience God's justifying act and enter into a right relationship with Him. In the previous paragraphs we saw that we are justified because of our union with Christ. Here we are justified through faith. Both statements are true because it is through faith that we are united to Christ, so that His life becomes our life, His death becomes our death, and His righteousness our righteousness. All the objective work of Christ for us is applied to us and received by us through faith in Him.

When it comes to justification through faith, Paul is like a dog with a bone. He will not let go. He keeps hammering away on the truth that justification is through faith, not works. In verse 28, for example, he says, "For we maintain that a man is justified by faith apart from observing the law." He devotes the entire fourth chapter of Romans to this truth.

Or consider just a short paragraph in his letter to the Galatians (2:15-16):

We who are Jews by birth and not "Gentile sinners" know that a man is not justified by observing the law, but by faith in Jesus Christ. So we, too, have put our faith in Christ Jesus that we may be justified by faith in Christ and not by observing the law, because by observing the law no one will be justified.

Notice his repetition of the word *justified*. I often jokingly say that Paul's work would not get past my editor, because editors by nature are highly allergic to frequent use of the same word. But Paul had a point to make, and he wanted to be sure the Galatian believers didn't miss it: We are justified by faith in Jesus Christ and not by observing the Law. And this is the same message he develops more fully in Romans 3 through 4.

If faith is so important, so essential, to our being justified, we need to explore more fully the nature of faith. To help us do this, let's take a look at Romans 10:13-15:

"Everyone who calls on the name of the Lord will be saved." How, then, can they call on the one they have not believed in? And how can they believe in the one of whom they have not heard? And how can they hear without someone preaching to them? And how can they preach unless they are sent? As it is written, "How beautiful are the feet of those who bring good news!"

Note the four verbs in this passage: *call, believe, hear,* and *preach*. These four words, taken in reverse order, help us understand the nature of faith. First someone *preaches* a message. In the light of Acts 8:4, we should understand "preach" to cover every instance of sharing the gospel, whether to an individual or to an audience. What is it that is preached? Romans 10:17

says, "Consequently, faith comes from hearing the message, and the message is heard through the word of Christ." In the context of Romans, the message is obviously the gospel that Paul has already explained in great detail.

As someone shares the gospel, a person *hears* it. Paul's simple logic is beautiful. Before a person can believe, he or she must first hear the message of the gospel. Faith must have content. It is not a leap in the dark, hoping all will turn out well. Faith involves hearing and understanding the message. Faith is directed toward a body of truth—namely, the gospel.

I don't want to speculate on how much of the gospel a person must hear and understand in order to exercise faith, but as a minimum it will include the truth that "Christ died for our sins according to the Scriptures" (1 Corinthians 15:3). At the same time it must be simple enough for a child to understand.

After a person hears the message, he or she must *believe;* that is, believe that the gospel message is true and applicable to his or her situation. Note, however, that Paul doesn't stop at merely believing the message. He writes of "believing in" the One of whom they have heard. The object of our faith is not the mere content of the message, but the One whom the message is about.

Finally, as we believe in Jesus, we *call* on Him. We can label this last step of "calling" embracing Christ, or trusting in Him alone for our salvation. Scripture uses several words for calling on Christ—for example, *receive* (see John 1:12), *believe in* (see John 3:16), and *trust* (see Romans 4:5). The Puritans had a quaint expression for it. They spoke of "closing" with Christ, using that word the way we use it to refer to closing on a home.

I like to say that exercising faith involves *renunciation* and *reliance.* The Scriptures teach that trusting in Christ necessarily involves renouncing any trust in our own good works, whatever form they might take. (See, for example, Romans 4:4-5; 10:1-4; Galatians 2:15-16; Ephesians 2:8-9.) Then we must rely entirely on the perfect righteousness of Jesus Christ. Paul speaks of "the man who does not work but trusts God who justifies the wicked" (Romans 4:5). There is an absolute antithesis between trusting, even to the smallest degree, in our own works of goodness and trusting or relying entirely on the righteousness of Christ for our justification. This complete renunciation of any confidence in our own goodness and total reliance upon Christ and His work for us is beautifully captured in Augustus Toplady's famous hymn *Rock of Ages:*

> Nothing in my hands I bring,
> Simply to the cross I cling.

The same attitude of renunciation and reliance is also well expressed in Edward Mote's hymn *The Solid Rock:*

> My hope is built on nothing less
> Than Jesus' blood and righteousness;
> No merit of my own I claim,[4]
> But wholly lean on Jesus' name.

As we come to Christ, then, empty-handed, claiming no merit of our own, but clinging by faith to His blood and righteousness, we are justified. We pass immediately from a state of condemnation and spiritual death to a state of pardon, acceptance, and the sure hope of eternal life. Our sins are blotted out, and we are "clothed" with the righteousness of Jesus Christ. In our standing before God, we will never be more righteous, even in heaven, than we were the day we trusted Christ, or we are now. Obviously in our daily experience we fall far short of the perfect righteousness God requires. But because He has imputed to us the perfect righteousness of His Son, He now sees us as being just as righteous as Christ Himself.

PEACE WITH GOD

What's more, Paul says, "since we have been justified through faith, we have peace with God through our Lord Jesus Christ" (Romans 5:1). This is an objective peace. The war is over. The alienation and divine displeasure toward us because of our sin have been removed. We are no longer objects of wrath. We have peace with God whether we realize it or not. However, to the extent that we understand and believe the truth regarding justification, we will experience a subjective peace—that is, a sense of peace within our souls. We will know that we have been brought from a state of condemnation and the prospect of eternal judgment into a state of forgiveness and favor with God.

I well remember the night I trusted Christ as an eighteen-year-old. Outwardly I was a model teenager but not a Christian, even though I knew the gospel message. One night alone in my bed I asked Christ to be my Savior. Immediately I had peace in my soul, brought to me by the Holy Spirit. But that experiential peace was possible only because Christ had made peace with God for me through His death on the cross.

A POINT-IN-TIME EVENT

In Romans 5:1, Paul speaks of our justification in the past tense: "We have been justified." Justification is a point-in-time experience that occurs the moment a person trusts in Christ as Savior. I realize the precise moment of justification is not identifiable to many people who grew up in Christian homes, and whose faith in Christ was a growing experience. If such is your situation, I would ask: Are you trusting in Christ as your Savior today? If so, there was a time, known only to God, when you were justified; you were declared righteous before Him. You can have confidence in this fact.

Justification, however, is not just a point-in-time event that passes into our memory bank as a pleasant experience of the past. Rather it is a point-in-time event that has eternal ongoing benefit for us. In Romans 5:2, Paul writes that "through [our Lord Jesus Christ] we have gained access by faith into this grace in which we now stand." The grace Paul refers to is the grace of justification, and he says we now, today, *stand* in that grace. That is, by His grace, we have gained the status or standing of justification, and we will forever remain in that standing. It can never change. We will for the remainder of our lives and throughout eternity stand before God justified, declared righteous in His sight because He has given to us the righteousness of Christ.

A point-in-time event resulting in a continuing, permanent change of status is not all that unusual. In the case of child adoption, there is a point in time when the child becomes the legal son or daughter of the adopting parents. The child receives the parents' family name and enters into a lifelong status as the child of those parents. A similar thing occurs with immigrants who become naturalized citizens of our country. Though a legal pronouncement is made on a certain day declaring them to be citizens of the United States, this is a point-in-time experience in which they continue to "stand" the rest of their lives.

So it is with our justification. There was a point in time when we trusted in Christ and were by faith united to Him so that His death became our death, His obedience our obedience,

His righteousness our righteousness. If this is true of you, then the most important question you could ever ask—How can I, a sinful human being, come into a right relationship with a holy and just God?—has been answered. You stand before God today and are forevermore declared righteous by Him. You now possess that right relationship with God.

A PRESENT REALITY

Unfortunately, many believers do not live as if justification is a permanent, abiding state. They have divorced their hope of eternal life in heaven from their relationship with God today. They think as if they will "put on" Christ's robe of righteousness at death. Meanwhile, in this life they draw their sense of God's acceptance from their most recent performance of Christian duties or their avoidance of certain sins. Their "robe of righteousness" for daily living is not that which they have from Christ, but one that they have stitched together by their own performance. They do not live in the here and now as if they are righteous in the sight of God solely because they have the righteousness of Christ.

By contrast, the apostle Paul lived in a continuous state of conscious justification. In Galatians 2:20 he wrote, "The life I [now] live in the body, I live by faith in the Son of God, who loved me and gave himself for me."[5] In the context of verses 15 through 21, Paul is speaking of his faith in Christ for justification. But it is not justification as simply a past event. Rather, in using the word *now* he is speaking of his present daily experience of living in a state of justification. As George Smeaton wrote on this verse, "Obviously, this is not the language of faith for attaining justification, but the language of a man already justified, and glorying in a sense of acceptance and the experience of grace."[6]

It is important that we see what Paul was saying by his use of the word *now*. For Paul, justification was not only a point-in-time event that occurred in the past, but it was a *present reality* in which he rejoiced every day. Paul did what we should do. He renounced any confidence in his own performance or, for that matter, any dismay over his lack of performance. Instead, by faith he looked to Jesus Christ and His righteousness for his sense of being in right standing with God today and tomorrow, and throughout eternity.

Early in the twentieth century, the great Princeton Seminary theologian B. B. Warfield wrote:

> There is nothing in us or done by us, at any stage of our earthly development, because of which we are acceptable to God. We must always be accepted for Christ's sake, or we cannot ever be accepted at all. This is not true of us only when we believe. It is just as true after we have believed. It will continue to be true as long as we live. Our need of Christ does not cease with our believing; nor does the nature of our relation to Him or to God through Him ever alter, no matter what our attainments in Christian graces or our achievements in behavior may be. It is always on His "blood and righteousness" alone that we can rest.[7]

Do you grasp what Warfield was saying? There is nothing you will ever do that makes you acceptable to God. You must be accepted for Christ's sake, not only when you believe, but for all of your life. Regardless of how much you grow in Christ, you will never arrive at a point when your Christian character or conduct will make you acceptable to God. You will always be dependent on the perfect righteousness of Christ. God will accept nothing else. That is why justification must be for us not only a past event, but a present reality.

As we come to the end of this chapter, take some time to prayerfully ask yourself these questions:

- Do I have a right relationship with God based on the imputed righteousness of Jesus Christ?
- Am I trusting in Jesus Christ alone for my salvation, or am I to some degree relying on my own morality and religious duties?
- If I know that I am justified through faith in Christ, do I enjoy the reality of it in my daily experience, or do I look to my own performance for my acceptance with God?

Throughout this book I have continually referred to the unsearchable riches of Christ. Think of those riches as represented by Christ standing with cupped hands filled to overflowing with fourteen-carat diamonds, representing His infinitely perfect righteousness. You stand beside Him with a fist full of baubles and trinkets from the local toy store, representing your own righteousness. Which do you want to present to God as the basis of gaining or maintaining your acceptance with Him? Your baubles or Christ's diamonds? I pray that you make the right choice.

PAUL'S GREAT EXCHANGE

If anyone else thinks he has reasons to put confidence
in the flesh, I have more: circumcised on the eighth day,
of the people of Israel, of the tribe of Benjamin, a
Hebrew of Hebrews; in regard to the law, a Pharisee; as
for zeal, persecuting the church; as for legalistic righteousness, faultless. (PHILIPPIANS 3:4-6)

Saul of Tarsus was the type of person many churches would
be eager to have on their board. His credentials were impres-
sive. In contemporary language they might look like this:

- Baptized (or dedicated) in the church as an infant
- From a family that traces its religious heritage all the
  way back to the Mayflower Pilgrims
- Very devout and scrupulous in practicing his faith
- A zealous church worker
- Character and conduct above reproach

Furthermore, we learn from Acts 22:28 that Paul (as he was
also called) was born a Roman citizen, indicating that his father

(at least, and perhaps several generations before him) was a Roman citizen, even though Jewish. This suggests that Paul came from a family of the social elite in Tarsus. And his religious credentials were outstanding, thoroughly trained as he was in Jewish law under Gamaliel, one of the leading teachers of that day.

All of Paul's past was something to be grateful for. There was nothing to be ashamed of. Even in persecuting the church he thought he was working for God. Yet there came a time in Paul's life when he "threw it all overboard." Why do I use that particular expression? You recognize it as a nautical phrase, and the reason I use it is because of Paul's use of the word *loss* in Philippians 3:7-8:

> But whatever was to my profit I now consider loss for the sake of Christ. What is more, I consider everything a loss compared to the surpassing greatness of knowing Christ Jesus my Lord, for whose sake I have lost all things. I consider them rubbish, that I may gain Christ.

LOSS OF CARGO

There is only one other place in the New Testament where *loss* is used, and that is in Luke's description of Paul's disastrous voyage to Rome that Paul had experienced only months before writing his letter to the Philippians. Acts 27 is a record of that voyage, and in the account Paul speaks twice of the *loss* of cargo suffered because of a violent storm.

In those days, when a ship was caught in a violent storm, as a last resort the crew would throw cargo and tackle overboard in order to lighten the shipload. This would cause the ship to ride higher in the water, diminishing the danger of being swamped by the high waves washing over the deck. Obviously, however, such action would entail great loss to the ship owner or captain.

Only one other scriptural account speaks of the loss of a ship's cargo: Jonah 1:5. In such heavy seas as Paul and Jonah experienced, the cargo actually became dangerous. To keep it on board jeopardized not only the ship, but the crew and passengers as well.

In both instances, the masters of the ships were faced with a difficult choice: throw the cargo overboard and suffer its loss, but hopefully save the ship; or keep the cargo on board and risk losing everything—cargo, ship, and the lives of passengers and crew.

PAUL'S LOSS

In Philippians 3, then, Paul speaks of the loss of his religious credentials as he earlier spoke of the loss of the ship's cargo. The analogy of the loss of ship's cargo to Paul's own religious experience is this: Any confidence in one's own religious attainments in the issue of salvation is not only useless, but downright dangerous. Though Paul had nothing to be ashamed of and much to be thankful for, those very things could keep him from eternal salvation.

Here, however, the analogy to losing a ship's cargo ends. A ship's crew (especially the captain) would throw the cargo overboard with deep regret because doing so meant great financial loss. I am a businessman at heart, and I identify with those ship owners every time I read the accounts of Jonah and Paul's disastrous voyages. They were what we would today call small-business owners, and I think of their great financial loss from jettisoning their cargo, especially when there was no marine insurance to cover the loss. If I had been captain of one of those vessels, the choice between loss of cargo and loss of my life would have been a no-brainer. Still, I would have chosen with great regret.

For Paul, however, there was no regret, none whatsoever. In fact he speaks of his "cargo" of religious background and attainments as rubbish (see verse 8). Probably a more accurate and descriptive word for rubbish in verse 8 is *garbage*—table scraps or the kind of stuff you put down your garbage disposal. When I served in the U.S. Navy, our ship had a garbage chute at the very stern of the ship. After meal cleanup, the garbage was dumped down the chute to be lost in the depth of the ocean. Contrary to regret at throwing cargo overboard, there was no regret about the garbage. We were glad to get rid of it.

PAUL'S DISCOVERY

Paul had come to the conclusion that his religious background was not only dangerous to his spiritual safety, but in a sense, it was no more than garbage—something to be deliberately dumped down the chute. Why? Because he had discovered something far more valuable. He had discovered the righteousness that comes from God through faith in Jesus Christ (see Philippians 3:9).

Paul had previously counted on his religious attainments as the basis of his acceptance with God. Like his fellow Jews, he had sought to establish his own righteousness through keeping the Law (see Romans 10:3-4). But there came a time, possibly during his three days of blindness and fasting in Damascus (see Acts 9:7-9), when he realized that his efforts to become righteous through law-keeping were going nowhere. They kept him from the only means of salvation God has provided. As he realized more clearly the perfect righteousness that God has provided through His Son, Jesus Christ, he saw his own efforts to be righteous as no more than garbage to be dumped overboard.

So Paul made what I call his *great exchange*. He exchanged his own righteousness for the perfect righteousness of Jesus Christ. He not only threw his own righteousness overboard, he regarded it as mere garbage compared to the surpassing greatness of knowing Christ Jesus as his Savior and being credited with His righteousness. He exchanged the garbage of his goodness for the unsearchable riches of Christ.

Of course Paul could make his great exchange only because God had already made *the* great exchange described in 2 Corinthians 5:21: "God made him who had no sin to be sin for us, so that in him [that is, through union with Christ] we might become the righteousness of God." God laid our sin upon Christ in order that He might lay Christ's righteousness upon us.

Note the subtle wording. Paul exchanged his *righteousness* through keeping the Law for Christ's righteousness that comes by faith. Yet in 2 Corinthians 5:21, God exchanges our *sin* for Christ's righteousness. What do we learn from this? We see that our own efforts at righteousness are, at bottom, only sin because they fail to measure up to the perfect righteousness required by God's Law. To use the food metaphor, they are not just leftovers to be used tomorrow; they are scraps to be thrown out as garbage.

Let's return to the merchant ship analogy. Paul likely traveled on a grain ship used to transport grain from Egypt to Rome. Suppose one of those ships is in port, ready to take on a cargo of wheat, when the ship owner learns that he has an opportunity to transport a load of gold worth many times more than a cargo of grain, which would produce for him a much greater profit. What will he do? Will he say, "I can't take the gold. My ship is a grain ship"? Not at all. In that situation he disdains the grain because he has the opportunity to carry something far more valuable. So the captain makes his own great exchange. He exchanges the opportunity to transport wheat for the far more profitable opportunity to carry gold.

So we actually have to look at two scenarios in the merchant marine world to get to a proper analogy of what Paul is saying to us in Philippians. On the one hand, there is the picture of the ship in the storm in which our cargo of human goodness becomes dangerous if it keeps us from looking to Christ as our only hope for becoming right with God. But the second scenario of disdaining the wheat in order to carry the gold teaches us that even our best performance is no better than garbage when compared to the righteousness of Christ. It is not that our performance may not be good. Quite the contrary. In Paul's case his religious background and attainments were outstanding. But when he compared it with the absolutely perfect righteousness of Christ, he dismissed it as mere garbage.

A MIRACLE OF GRACE

I believe that human morality, rather than flagrant sin, is the greatest obstacle to the gospel today. If you ask the average law-abiding person why he expects to go to heaven, the answer will be some form of "because I've been good." The rich young ruler (see Matthew 19:16-20), the prodigal son's older brother (see Luke 15:28-30), and the Pharisee praying in the temple (see Luke 18:9-12) all had this in common: They were confident of their own goodness. Their attitude is replicated throughout our society. And the more religious a person is, the more difficult it is for that person to realize his or her need for the righteousness of Jesus Christ.

I once read a story about two men who happened to be kneeling side by side at the communion rail of an English church. One was a former convict who had served time and was now out of prison. The other was the judge who had sentenced him to prison years before.

After the service the minister asked the judge, "Did you recognize the man kneeling beside you?"

"Yes I did," replied the judge. "That was a miracle of grace."

"You mean that a man you sentenced to prison should be kneeling beside you?"

"No, not at all," said the judge. "The miracle is that I should be kneeling beside him. You see, that man knew clearly he was a sinner in need of a Savior. But I was brought up in a religious home, have lived a decent, moral life, and have served my community. It is much more difficult for someone such as I to recognize his need for a Savior. I am the miracle of grace."

How do you respond to Paul's personal experience? Do you identify with it in the sense of having come to the place where you have made your own "great exchange"? Have you renounced any confidence in your own religious experience and trusted solely in Christ's blood and righteousness? Perhaps you are somewhat like the English judge who grew up in a highly moral and religious family. You've always been good and essentially blameless in the eyes of other people. That's nothing to be ashamed of. But if your hope of eternal life is based on that goodness, then your "cargo" of religion has actually become dangerous to you. It will keep you from heaven.

Suppose, however, you identify to some degree with the former prisoner. You may think your sin is too great to be forgiven. But the prisoner kneeling beside the judge and the penitent thief hanging on the cross are witnesses to the fact that the blood of Christ can indeed cleanse us from *all* sin. Whether you identify with the judge or the former prisoner, you too can be a miracle of grace.

WHAT ABOUT US?

What about the rest of us, however? What about those of us who have trusted in Christ? Does Paul's personal story have any relevance for us? By all means. All of us have a natural drift toward a performance-based relationship with God. We know we are saved by grace through faith—not by works (see Ephesians 2:8-9), but we somehow get the idea that we earn blessings by our works. After throwing overboard our works as a means to salvation, we want to drag them back on board as a means of maintaining favor with God. Or, to use the food analogy, instead of seeing our own righteousness as table scraps to be dumped down the garbage chute, we see it as leftovers to be used later to earn answers to prayer.

We need to learn and remind ourselves every day that God's favor—His blessings and answers to prayer—comes to us not on the basis of our works, but on the basis of the infinite merit of Jesus Christ. Is there any place in the Christian life, then, for the practice of the spiritual disciplines, for obedience to God, and for sacrificial service to Him? Absolutely! And as we continue to look at Paul's story we'll see what that place is.

PRESSING ON

There is no doubt that Paul was just as diligent and zealous, probably more so, after he trusted Christ as he was before. We have only to continue reading his words in Philippians 3:12-14:

> Not that I have already obtained all this, or have
> already been made perfect, but I press on to take hold
> of that for which Christ Jesus took hold of me.
> Brothers, I do not consider myself yet to have taken
> hold of it. But one thing I do: Forgetting what is
> behind and straining toward what is ahead, I press on
> toward the goal to win the prize for which God has
> called me heavenward in Christ Jesus.

Note the two intense expressions Paul uses: *press on* (verses
12 and 14), and *straining toward* (verse 13). The word translated
press on is the same word that is translated *persecuting* in
Philippians 3:6. In fact, that is the most common use of the word
in the New Testament. As Paul uses it in verses 12 and 14, it has
the idea of pursuing so as to lay hold of a prize. The idea of *straining toward* is very graphic. It is the picture of a runner straining
every nerve and muscle as he strives to cross the finish line.

However, the underlying motivation behind Paul's zeal in
verse 6 is dramatically different from that in verses 12 through
14. In verse 6 it is the zeal of self-righteousness. In verses 12
through 14 it is the zeal of a man exulting in the perfect righteousness of Christ and consequently yearning to be all that
God intended him to be (expressed by Paul as taking hold of
that for which Christ Jesus took hold of him).

There is a direct correlation between faith in the righteousness of Christ and zeal in the cause of Christ. The more a person
counts as loss his own righteousness and lays hold by faith of the
righteousness of Christ, the more he will be motivated to live and
work for Christ. The same Christian activity can be either an
expression of our own righteousness that we think earns favor

with God, or it can be an expression of love and gratitude because we already have His favor through the righteousness of Christ.

As we come to the close of this chapter, let me ask you two questions:

- Are you trusting in the righteousness of Christ alone as the basis of your right standing with God, or are you still depending on your religious performance, even to a small degree?
- Are you, if you have clearly trusted in Christ alone for your salvation, still clinging to the idea that you must now earn God's favor in this life by your own performance?

Obedience and good works are definitely important to the Christian life. The entire New Testament clearly affirms that. But if we try to make them meritorious, earning for us the hope of eternal life or even God's favor in this life, they become dangerous cargo, mere garbage. May we clearly see that in the unsearchable riches of Christ and in the right standing with God that comes from those riches, we have both the assurance of eternal life and God's favor in this life.

CHAPTER ELEVEN

THE GIFT OF GOD

Y ou cannot read closely the apostle Paul's explanation of the gospel in Romans 3 through 4 without realizing how important faith is to the message. Right from the beginning he tells us that this righteousness from God by which we are justified comes through faith in Jesus Christ (see 3:22). Beginning at this verse and continuing through chapter 4 he uses the noun *faith* and its equivalent verb *believe* over twenty times.

In fact, if there is any one truth that Paul seems to feel strongly about, it is the absolute antithesis between justification by faith and justification by keeping the Law. This is why I said earlier that faith must involve a complete renunciation of trust in one's own goodness (keeping the Law), as well as a total reliance on Jesus Christ and His righteousness.

The question arises then: How do we get faith? Does it come simply as an intellectual response to the gospel message? Or do those of us who share the gospel with others need to master the art of persuasion, or learn the technique of "closing the sale"? How does one get faith?

The short answer is that faith is the gift of God. It has to be. There's an old adage that "a man convinced against his will is of the same opinion still." Have you ever tried to convince someone to change his or her mind when that person didn't want to change? You may marshal well-documented reasons and unassailable facts, but unless that person is receptive to you, he or she will not change. They just mentally "dig in their heels." Now if this is true in the ordinary affairs of life, how much more is it true in the spiritual realm?

OUR SPIRITUAL BONDAGE

Paul's writings are filled with dismal descriptions of our spiritual condition before we became believers. Ephesians 2:1-3 is one of the most complete.

> As for you, you were dead in your transgressions and
> sins, in which you used to live when you followed the
> ways of this world and of the ruler of the kingdom of
> the air, the spirit who is now at work in those who
> are disobedient. All of us also lived among them at
> one time, gratifying the cravings of our sinful nature
> and following its desires and thoughts. Like the rest,
> we were by nature objects of wrath.

The first thing Paul says is that we were dead. Of course he is speaking about spiritual death. As such, we were totally unresponsive to the God of Scripture. We may have been religious, but we were still dead. Remember the story of Saul of Tarsus in the last chapter? No one today could claim to be more religious than he, yet he was spiritually dead.

Spiritually dead people cannot receive and embrace the gospel. As Paul said in 1 Corinthians 2:14, "The man without the Spirit does not accept the things that come from the Spirit of God, for they are foolishness to him, and he cannot understand them, because they are spiritually discerned." Does this mean that unbelievers cannot understand the facts of the gospel? No—it means they cannot sense their own need of it and embrace it. As long as we were spiritually dead we could not just "decide" to believe the gospel and trust in Jesus Christ.

Following the overall description of our condition as spiritually dead, Paul describes in greater detail what that spiritual deadness looks like (verses 2-3).

The first thing Paul says is that we followed the ways of the world. The word *world* is often used in the Bible as a shorthand expression for the sum total of human society that is in opposition to God. It consists of refined religious people such as Saul of Tarsus (and thousands of church members today), as well as the most vile and despicable people we readily identify as "sinners." Here are some descriptive expressions of people of the world:

There is no one righteous, not even one;
there is no one who understands,
no one who seeks God. . . .
there is no one who does good,
not even one. . . .
There is no fear [reverence] of God before their eyes.
(Romans 3:10-12,18)

This is the world. Its attitude toward God varies all the way from indifference to hostility, but the bottom line is, it does not seek God. And this is the world we followed.

Second, Paul says we followed "the ruler of the kingdom of the air, the spirit who is now at work in those who are disobedient" (verse 2). This is a reference to Satan, the Devil. We don't like to think that we were followers of the Devil, but that is what the Bible says. This does not mean we were as wicked as we could be, because, after all, as Paul said elsewhere, "Satan himself masquerades as an angel of light" (2 Corinthians 11:14). What it does mean is that Satan blinded us to the gospel. As Paul again said, "The god of this age has blinded the minds of unbelievers, so that they cannot see the light of the gospel of the glory of Christ, who is the image of God" (2 Corinthians 4:4). And then in Colossians 1:13, he wrote that God "rescued us from the dominion of darkness [that is, Satan's kingdom] and brought us into the kingdom of the Son he loves."

Before God delivered us from Satan's dominion we were his captives. We could not see the light of the gospel. This speaks of a spiritual—not mental—inability. We were spiritually blind, unable to recognize our need of the Savior or to see God's gracious provision of Him.

Next, Paul tells us that we were gratifying the cravings of our sinful nature (see Ephesians 2:3). Paul describes this nature more specifically in Romans 8:7-8: "The sinful mind is hostile to God. It does not submit to God's law, nor can it do so. Those controlled by the sinful nature cannot please God." Note the absolute negatives Paul uses. Our sinful nature *cannot* submit to God's Law; it *cannot* please God. In Romans 6:17, he describes us as having been slaves to sin; that is, in bondage to our sinful nature.

It is difficult for decent, upright Americans to accept the fact that we are by nature hostile to God, that we cannot please Him. This is because we have confused general American morality, plus a dose of Sunday church attendance, with obedience to God's Law. Most Americans have never been seriously confronted with the exceedingly high standard of God's eternal Law. When they are, they typically reveal their underlying hostility to it.

Let's summarize for a moment: We were spiritually dead, enmeshed in a culture totally opposed to God, under the dominion of Satan, and slaves of our own sinful natures. And apart from a supernatural work of God in our lives, we were helpless to do anything about our condition.

ALIVE WITH CHRIST

Paul is fond of painting an absolutely dismal picture of our condition and then saying, "But here is God's remedy." He does it in Romans 3:20-21 and Titus 3:3-7, as well as in Ephesians 2:1-5, where he says that although we were dead in our transgressions and sins, God made us alive with Christ. It is God who gives us spiritual life. We could not make ourselves spiritually alive any more than a dead person can make himself alive.

When Lazarus lay dead in the tomb he could not decide to come to life again. In fact, Lazarus could not even respond to Jesus' call, "Lazarus, come out!" unless with that call Jesus gave him life (see John 11:1-44 for the complete story). Lazarus's condition, as he lay dead in the tomb, is a picture of our spiritual predicament. We can hear the call of the gospel a hundred times, but unless that call is accompanied by the life-giving power of the Holy Spirit, we can no more respond to it than Lazarus could respond to a vocal call from Jesus.

I know it is difficult for us to accept the fact that we could not just decide to trust Christ in much the same way we might decide to buy more life insurance. The truth is, we did decide to trust Christ, but the reason we made that decision is that God had first made us spiritually alive. This is part of the good news. God comes to us when we are spiritually dead, when we don't even realize our condition, and gives us the spiritual ability to see our plight and to see in Christ the solution. God doesn't just come partway to meet us in our need. He comes all the way. When we were dead,

He made us alive in Christ Jesus. And the first act of that new life is to turn in faith to Jesus.

THE NEW BIRTH

We see this necessity of the Spirit's work in giving us faith in Jesus' conversation with the Pharisee Nicodemus (see John 3:1-21). In verse 3 Jesus says emphatically[1] that "no one can see the kingdom of God unless he is born again." In verse 5 He says, "No one can enter the kingdom of God unless he is born of water and the Spirit." Finally, in verses 7 through 8 Jesus compares the sovereign action of the Spirit in bringing about the new birth with the sovereign and mysterious (to us) action of the wind.

What is Jesus saying to Nicodemus and to us? Notice that Jesus speaks not of permission to enter the kingdom, but of *inability* to enter it apart from a new birth. We all recognize the difference between the relationships of *may* to permission and *can* to ability. Here Jesus consistently uses the word *can*. We cannot — in other words, we do not have the ability to — enter the kingdom unless the Spirit of God gives us life through the new birth. We are born again, then, by a sovereign, monergistic (that is, the Spirit working alone) act of the Holy Spirit. Then, as a result of that new birth, we exercise the faith given to us and enter the kingdom of God.

It is in the light of the teaching of John 3:1-8 and Ephesians 2:1-5 — that faith comes as a result of spiritual life — that we should understand a Scripture such as Acts 16:14: "One of those listening was a woman named Lydia, a dealer in purple cloth from the city of Thyatira, who was a worshiper of God. The Lord opened her heart to respond to Paul's message."

What does it mean that the Lord opened Lydia's heart? It means that He made her spiritually alive, that she was born again. It means He removed the Satan-induced blindness from her mind so that she understood and embraced the gospel. It means that He delivered her from the kingdom of darkness, where she had been held captive, so that she could respond in faith. Note the sequence of events recorded by Luke. The Lord opened her heart; then she responded to Paul's message. She could not respond until God first opened her heart.

A New Thought

I realize that what I have been saying about the Spirit's work being necessary to produce faith is contrary to much current understanding. We are accustomed (and I was included in the "we" early in my Christian life) to believe that faith is generated in us solely by an intellectual understanding of the truth of the gospel and by a mere decision of our will to trust Christ. Then as a result of what *we* do on our own, God responds by giving us spiritual life or the new birth.

Though the notion that the regenerating work of the Holy Spirit (the new birth) precedes and results in our faith may be new to many of our day, it is in fact the historic teaching of the church since the sixteenth-century Reformation. Consider the words of Charles Wesley, the famous Methodist hymn writer of the eighteenth century:

Long my imprisoned spirit lay
Fast bound in sin and nature's night;
Thine eye diffused a quick'ning ray;

I woke, the dungeon flamed with light;
My chains fell off, my heart was free;
I rose, went forth, and followed thee.[2]

Note how Wesley saw his own heart imprisoned in sin, then the almighty work of the Spirit quickening (giving life to) him. Only then did he arise and follow Christ. What was true for Wesley is just as true for us today.

Obviously the Holy Spirit works through our human channels of evangelism. As we saw in chapter 9, "faith comes from hearing the message, and the message is heard through the word of Christ" (Romans 10:17). But our message is impotent apart from the working of the Holy Spirit, who both empowers the messenger and opens the heart of the listener as He did in the case of Lydia. Consider Paul's words to the Thessalonian believers: "Our gospel came to you not simply with words, but also with power, with the Holy Spirit and with deep conviction" (1 Thessalonians 1:5).

What resulted when Paul's message was accompanied by the powerful working of the Holy Spirit? The Thessalonians "turned to God from idols to serve the living and true God" (1:9).

The Thessalonians themselves believed. They exercised faith. God does not believe for us, but He does through His Spirit create spiritual life in us so that we can believe. Faith is a gift of God. It is part of the whole salvation package that God gives to us through the work of Christ for us and the work of the Holy Spirit in us. It is not our contribution, so to speak, to God's great plan of salvation. God does it all. Faith is part of the unsearchable riches of Christ.

AN ENCOURAGEMENT TO PRAYER

The realization that faith is the gift of God—not the result of the persuasion of the evangelist (and I use that term to refer to anyone who shares the gospel with another person)—should encourage us to pray with confidence. It means that no one, however hardened he or she may be, is beyond the regenerating, life-creating work of the Holy Spirit.

I think of some for whose salvation I pray regularly. One is stridently opposed to the gospel, wanting nothing to do with God. Another is happily indifferent, seeing no need of a Savior because he is a good, moral person. Others, at this point in our relationships, would be highly insulted to be told they need a Savior because, after all, they are both moral *and* religious. What hope is there for these people? It lies only in the sovereign, mysterious work of the Holy Spirit. And I pray regularly that He will work in the hearts of these people through the gospel message to create the faith they must have to believe in Christ.

GRATITUDE AND WORSHIP

Awareness that faith is the gift of God should also arouse a sense of profound gratitude and worship in our hearts. Not only did we not deserve God's gracious gift of salvation, we could not even take advantage of it apart from His prior working in our hearts. We were helpless to propitiate the wrath of God against our sin, and we were just as helpless to receive the fruit of that propitiation when it was offered to us. But God did not stop His work of salvation partway. Instead He gave us life when we were dead, gave us sight when we were blind, and gave us the faith to trust in Christ for our salvation. If we were to spend the rest of our lives doing nothing but saying "thank you" to God, we could still never sufficiently express to Him our gratitude for the gift of salvation, including the gift of faith by which we receive it.

After Paul had spent eleven chapters in Romans expounding the gospel in all its fullness and grandeur, he closed with a doxology, a note of praise to God: "For from him and through him and to him are all things. To him be the glory forever! Amen" (Romans 11:36).

The "all things" in Paul's mind would include the gift of faith. Do you want to grow in your own worship of God? That growth will be directly related to your understanding of the gospel in all its fullness, including the fact that the faith by which you believed was a gift from God.

CHAPTER TWELVE

CHILDREN OF GOD

Behold what manner of love the Father has bestowed
on us, that we should be called children of God!
(1 JOHN 3:1, NKJV)

M y wife has both an eye for beauty and an excitable personality. Frequently as we are driving along she will
startle me with an exclamation like "Look at that!" when she
has just seen a beautiful sunset, or a bank of snowy clouds, or
a gorgeous fall tree. If she were using the King James manner of
speech, she might say, "Behold, what a beautiful tree!" But
whether it's King James or contemporary English, in either case
she wants to get my attention.

Normally the word *behold* simply means "to see" or "to gaze
upon." But when it is used as an imperative verb, it carries the
strong idea of trying to get someone's attention. This is the sense
in which the apostle John uses it in 1 John 3:1. Only there he is
not saying, "Look at that!" but rather, "Think of this!" John is
saying, "Stop! Consider this astonishing fact: God loves us so
much that we are called His children. And it's true. We really are
His children!"

The NIV translators sought to capture the force of this amazing statement with the wording, "How great is the love the Father has lavished on us, that we should be called children of God! And that is what we are!" By the combined use of the superlative verb *lavish* and exclamation marks at the end of both sentences, they did their best to get us to stop and consider John's words.

So what is John saying? What is he so excited about? It is the truth that all believers are God's children. Think of that! If you have trusted in Jesus Christ as Savior, you are a child of God, a son or daughter of the Creator, Sustainer, and Ruler of the universe. I grant that oftentimes our circumstances, or even our behavior, can obscure the fact that we are children of God, but it is important that we keep this truth constantly before us. We'll see why as we move through this chapter. Meanwhile, what's the big deal? Why does John get so excited about a truth we often take for granted?

WHAT'S THE BIG DEAL?

What is so amazing about the fact that we believers are children of God? First of all, it's because of who we once were. Recall that in chapter 7, I used the analogy of a convicted serial killer on death row awaiting his execution. Perhaps a better analogy at this point is that of a condemned rebel who has tried to assassinate the king and overthrow his government. If that seems too strong a comparison to you, consider that every sin you commit is an act of rebellion against the sovereign authority of God, or, as someone has said, an act of cosmic treason.

So here we sit on death row, condemned as rebels, awaiting our execution. But instead of the death we deserve, we are made sons and daughters of the very King we have rebelled against. Instead of death, we get eternal life. Instead of wrath, we receive favor. Instead of eternal ruin, we are made heirs of God and co-heirs with Christ. All this happened without our doing a single thing to earn the King's favor, or any attempt on our part to make restitution for our rebellion. His Son has done it all for us.

In chapter 9 we saw that we are justified through faith in Jesus Christ. To review, justification is an act of God by which He forgives all our sins and accepts us as righteous in His sight because of the perfect righteousness of Christ imputed (or credited) to us by God and received by us through faith. Justification is a judicial declaration by God acting in His capacity as Supreme Judge. It is a legal act resulting in a legal standing.

However, we need something more than a legal standing if we are to live in the presence of God for all eternity. We need to be brought into a familial relationship with God. We need to become members of His family, and this is what has happened. God has not only justified us, He has made us family members. In theological terms this is called *adoption*. However, it is not adoption in the sense that we use that term today. It is much more. Here's why.

BORN OF GOD

A son or daughter in any human family is either born to or adopted by the parents. By definition, a child can't be both. But with God we are both *born of* Him and *adopted by* Him. Let's consider the former for a moment. The very idea is staggering, but that is what the Bible says: We are born again by His Spirit through His Word, the gospel (see John 3:8; 1 Peter 1:23).

John uses the expression *born of God* seven times in his first letter (1 John 2:29; 3:9 twice; 4:7; 5:1; 5:4; 5:18). All seven refer to evidence of new life in Christ. To become a child of God, then, refers not only to a new relationship, but also to a new life. In the words of Peter, we participate in, or become partakers of, the divine nature (see 2 Peter 1:4). This in no way suggests that we become "little gods," but it does mean that the supernatural life of Christ begins to invade and permeate our innermost being.

Just as parents pass on certain physical and personality traits to their natural-born children, so traits of divine life are passed on to those born of God. Thus John can say that those born of God do what is right, love others, believe in Jesus, and cease to practice sin. These are all family traits that show up to some degree in everyone born of God. And it is why, to return to our analogy, God is not afraid to take the serial killer from his cell on death row into His family home. He has been born again. He no longer has the heart of a serial killer.

ADOPTED BY GOD

The Bible also speaks of our being adopted by God. Consider the following (the *New International Version,* unlike the *New American Standard Bible,* does not actually use the word *adoption* in these particular passages):

> For you did not receive a spirit that makes you a slave again to fear, but you received the Spirit of sonship ["adoption as sons," NASB]. And by him we cry, "*Abba,* Father." (Romans 8:15)

> But when the time had fully come, God sent his Son, born of a woman, born under law, to redeem those

under law, that we might receive the full rights of sons ["adoption," NASB]. Because you are sons, God sent the Spirit of his Son into our hearts, the Spirit who calls out, *"Abba,* Father." (Galatians 4:4-6)

What does it mean to be adopted as sons by God? For one thing, it means that we have been brought into a close personal relationship with Him. Remember, we were rebels on death row, awaiting our execution date. But when God pardoned us, He adopted us and brought us into His royal family.

What's more, we have confident and ready access to Him. He gives us the privilege of addressing Him as "Abba, Father." *Abba* was the word for "father" in the Aramaic language of Jews in Paul's day. It was a term of intimate endearment toward and confidence in the one so addressed. It was the term used by Jesus in the Garden of Gethsemane when He prayed to His Father that the cup of wrath might be taken from Him (see Mark 14:36). And Paul tells us that because of our adoption as sons we can address the eternal God of the universe—the One whom we have rebelled against—as "Abba, Father."

There is still more meaning in the term *adoption.* The NIV translation of Galatians 4:5, "that we might receive the *full rights of sons*" (emphasis added) speaks of privileges accompanying our adoption. The adoption Paul refers to is not that of an infant or small child, as is typical in our culture today. In Jewish culture it would refer to the status of those who had advanced from minors to full-grown sons. Thus, the "full rights of sons" is probably a good rendition of what Paul was saying. In Roman culture adoption would refer to the practice of wealthy but childless couples' adopting a worthy young man to be their heir and carry on the family name.

In either case, think of what that means. As far as status is concerned, the brand-new believer comes into the family of God with the full rights of an adult son. Practically speaking, this new believer is a spiritual babe and needs discipling from more mature Christians. But at the same time he or she has all the rights and privileges of full-grown sons. So whether we are babes in Christ or mature believers, we all have the same privilege of addressing God as "Abba, Father."

A good sense of what it means to receive the full rights of sons can be seen in the restoration of the prodigal son upon his return from the far country (see Luke 15:22-24). The father orders the servants to quickly bring the best robe and put it on him, to place a ring on his finger, and sandals on his feet. In the custom of that day, the robe would have been a status symbol, the ring probably an indication of family authority, and the sandals a sign of sonship. He then orders the killing of the fattened calf, which would have been reserved for only the most special of occasions.

The contrast could not be greater. From a mere hireling, hungry, bedraggled, and feeding pigs, this young man is immediately restored to a position of dignity, honor, and full acceptance. He even becomes the guest of honor at a feast of celebration. Though this is not the intent of the parable, it can help us to see what it means to receive the privilege of adoption as full-grown sons.

Remember again that we were rebels, objects of God's wrath, and on death row. We should never lose sight of this fact, for it is the tremendous contrast between what we once were and what we have become by His grace that makes our sonship so amazing. We too have been redeemed from slavery to sin and Satan, have been clothed with the robe of Christ's perfect righteousness, and have been given status as sons in the royal household. No wonder John begins his remarkable statement about our sonship with "Behold." Think of this!

GOD OUR FATHER

What does it mean in everyday life that God is our Father? I recognize that some people have not had a good relationship with their human fathers. For them the very word *father* brings up images of harshness, cruelty, abuse, unfaithfulness, or perhaps just plain indifference. I remember the words of one student: "If God is like my father, I want nothing to do with God."

Happily, God is not like his father. His father was indeed harsh and demanding, but God "is gracious and compassionate, slow to anger and rich in love" (Psalm 145:8). Or consider Psalm 147:3-4:

> He heals the brokenhearted
> and binds up their wounds.
> He determines the number of the stars
> and calls them each by name.

Note the contrasting views of God in these two verses. The same God who by His mighty power creates and sustains the stars in their courses is at the same time the tenderhearted God who heals the broken and binds up their wounds. The Psalms are replete with such fatherly images of God.

Whether we have a father whom we respect and cherish or one who is worthy to be despised, we should never form our view of God from any human pattern. Rather, we should go to the Bible to get a true picture of our heavenly Father.

It is impossible in a book such as this to give a view of God that comes close to doing justice to the subject (which is why we need to go to the Bible). But let me suggest to you five fatherly responsibilities that God has assumed toward His children. For each I will give one passage of Scripture by way of illustration, which I hope will stimulate you to think of or find other Scriptures on this subject.

- God *provides* for us. "And my God will meet all your needs according to his glorious riches in Christ Jesus" (Philippians 4:19).
- God *protects* us. "Are not two sparrows sold for a penny? Yet not one of them will fall to the ground apart from the will of your Father. And even the very hairs of your head are all numbered. So don't be afraid; you are worth more than many sparrows" (Matthew 10:29-31).
- God *encourages* us. "You hear, O LORD, the desire of the afflicted; you encourage them, and you listen to their cry" (Psalm 10:17).
- God *comforts* us. "Praise be to the God and Father of our Lord Jesus Christ, the Father of compassion and the God of all comfort, who comforts us in all our troubles, so that we can comfort those in any trouble with the comfort we ourselves have received from God" (2 Corinthians 1:3-4).
- God *disciplines* us. "Our fathers disciplined us for a little while as they thought best; but God disciplines us for our good, that we may share in his holiness" (Hebrews 12:10).

I realize, and can testify from my own experience, that there are times when it does not seem as if God is doing any of these things. There are times when it seems as if He has forsaken us. At such times we need to lay hold of such promises as "Never will I leave you; never will I forsake you" (Hebrews 13:5). The fact is that God in His own inscrutable way is always at work to fulfill His role as our perfect heavenly Father.

THROUGH JESUS CHRIST

As we think of this relationship to God as our heavenly Father, we must always bear one important truth in mind. We have this relationship only through Jesus Christ. It is only because of our union with Christ that we are God's children and He is our Father. That is why Paul wrote, "In him [that is, through our union with Christ] and through faith in him we may approach God with freedom and confidence" (Ephesians 3:12; see also Ephesians 2:18; Hebrews 10:19-22).

Remember again, this book is about the unsearchable riches of Christ. Our status as children of God is one more glorious aspect of those inexhaustible riches. After John's exclamation that we should be called children of God, he adds, "And that is what we are!" It's as if he is saying, "It really is true!"

Well, it really is true. Do you believe it? Do you each day realize that you are a child of the heavenly King, or do you live more like the slave who asked for fifty cents to buy a sack of cornmeal? I hope this chapter has encouraged you to live as a full-grown child of God through Jesus Christ our Lord.

CHAPTER THIRTEEN

CONFIDENT ASSURANCE

D riving to the airport on a beautiful July morning, I felt good about the upcoming trip. The destination was my wife's home in Missouri. The routing was straightforward and seemingly stress free. I would fly to Denver, take the next flight to St. Louis, then catch a shuttle van to a small town in central Missouri where my wife would meet me and we would together drive to her family home.

The weather was great, and I looked forward to a relaxing, trouble-free trip. Was I in for a surprise! The entire trip began to unravel before I left Colorado Springs. Just as we were about to board the plane to Denver, our flight was canceled. Things went downhill from there. All three segments of the trip—the two flights as well as the shuttle—were fraught with delays and uncertainty. To top it off, I couldn't even reach my wife to let her know I would be late.

No one likes uncertainty, whether it's waiting for the results of a cancer biopsy or wondering whether you're going to make your connecting flight. Life is filled with uncertainties, some major, some minor. If you were to assign to them a stress level on a scale of one to ten, my flight delays would barely rate a one, while the results of a cancer biopsy would probably rate an eight or nine. But whether the issue is trivial or significant, we don't like uncertainty.

We saw in chapter 9 that having a right relationship with God is the most important question we can ever ask. That being true, it then follows that uncertainty over whether that relationship is real has to be the greatest uncertainty of all. If a cancer biopsy rates an eight or nine on our stress scale, then this question has to be off the chart.

God, however, does not want us to be uncertain about this issue. In fact, toward the end of his first letter, the apostle John wrote, "I write these things to you who believe in the name of the Son of God so that you may know that you have eternal life" (1 John 5:13). God wants us to *know* that we have eternal life. To some people the claim to know such a thing sounds presumptuous and arrogant. But if God wants us to know it, then it is only laying hold of what God wants us to enjoy.

How then can I know that I have eternal life, that I have indeed come into a right relationship with God? The Scriptures show us three means by which God assures us that we do have eternal life:

1. The promises of His Word
2. The witness of the Spirit in our hearts
3. The transforming work of the Spirit in our lives

THE PROMISES OF GOD

In chapter 11 we saw that faith is the gift of God. This may cause some to wonder whether God has truly given them the gift of faith, but that is the wrong question. Instead we should focus on the promises of God given without restriction in Scripture.

Consider, for example, the following gracious invitations and promises:

- "Come, all you who are thirsty, come to the waters; and you who have no money, come, buy and eat! Come, buy wine and milk without money and without cost" (Isaiah 55:1).
- "The Spirit and the bride say, 'Come!' And let him who hears say, 'Come!' Whoever is thirsty, let him come; and whoever wishes, let him take the free gift of the water of life" (Revelation 22:17).
- "All that the Father gives me will come to me, and whoever comes to me I will never drive away" (John 6:37).
- "Everyone who calls on the name of the Lord will be saved" (Romans 10:13).

Have you responded to the gracious invitations of Isaiah 55:1 and Revelation 22:17? One who is thirsty and one who has no money are simply metaphorical expressions for a person who realizes his or her need of a Savior. They are pictures of one who renounces any confidence at all in his own good works as the way to a right relationship with God. Does this describe you? Have you come to the place where you realize that you have no spiritual "money" with which to "buy" eternal life? Have you come as one who is spiritually thirsty, longing for that right relationship with God? Then God has promised that you will drink freely of the gift of the water of life.

Consider the promise of Romans 10:13. Have you called on the name of the Lord? Have you, in recognition of your own sinfulness, called on Jesus alone to be your Savior? Paul says all who do so will be saved.

Look at the gracious words of Jesus in John 6:37: "Whoever comes to me I will never drive away." If you have truly come to Him, sincerely asking Him to be your Savior, He will not drive you away.

Don't ask, "Do I have faith?" Ask rather, "Do I believe the promises of God?" If you believe those promises, it is because God *has* given you the gift of faith. Once in a while I get discouraged about my Christian life when God gives me a glimpse of the sinfulness in my heart. At those times I am tempted to ask, "Am I really a Christian?" When those rare occasions do occur, I go back to these promises, especially John 6:37. I know that I have come to Jesus and that He has promised me that He will not drive me away. Thus I regain and strengthen my assurance. We have to let the promises of God drive away our doubts. Our assurance of eternal life begins with believing the promises of God.

THE ACCUSATIONS OF SATAN

We should also realize that Satan is our accuser; in fact, that seems to be his primary strategy toward sincere believers. This is vividly illustrated in his accusation of the high priest, Joshua, recorded in Zechariah 3:1-4. Joshua is pictured as standing before the angel of the Lord, with Satan standing at his right hand to accuse him. But God rebukes Satan, takes away Joshua's filthy clothes (depicting his sin), and puts rich garments (symbolizing the robe of Christ's righteousness) on him. Perhaps Paul had this passage from Zechariah in mind when he wrote, "Who will bring any charge against those whom God has chosen? It is God who justifies" (Romans 8:33). God no longer allows Satan to accuse us before Him. In fact, we might say God has thrown Satan out of His heavenly courtroom.

However, although Satan can no longer accuse us before God, he accuses us to ourselves. He plants thoughts in our minds such as, "How could a person who is a Christian struggle with sin as much as you do?" What is our defense in such instances? It is not to ignore or minimize the seriousness of our sin. Rather it is to look at the cross of Christ and see Him bearing those sins in all their severity and ugliness in His body. It is to believe that "there is now no condemnation for those who are in Christ Jesus" (Romans 8:1), because Jesus was condemned in our place as our substitute.

So when you are troubled with uncertainty about your salvation, first recall the promises of God. Ask yourself, "Have I called on the name of the Lord? Have I come to Jesus? Have I come and called as one who is thirsty but has no money? Have I renounced any confidence in my own goodness and relied entirely on Jesus' blood and righteousness?" If you answer yes to those questions, then you need to rely on the promises of God.

THE WITNESS OF THE SPIRIT

Although the promises of God are the primary means by which He assures us of our salvation, they are not the only means. God knows our weaknesses, and He knows our tendencies to sometimes doubt whether those promises are true for us. Therefore, He has given us a second strong means of assurance, the witness of His Spirit.

Romans 8:15-16 is the key Scripture that assures us of this truth:

> For you did not receive a spirit that makes you a slave again to fear, but you received the Spirit of sonship. And by him we cry, "Abba, Father." The Spirit himself testifies with our spirit that we are God's children.

Here we get into an area that we cannot analyze or describe. How the Holy Spirit interacts with our human spirit is mysterious. It goes beyond the boundaries of our investigative abilities. However, though I cannot explain how the Spirit interacts with our spirits to give us assurance, I have certainly experienced it.

I still remember the night, now more than fifty years ago, when I asked Jesus to be my Savior. I was a teenage church member, but had no peace about my relationship with God. But the moment I asked Jesus Christ to be my Savior, my heart was flooded with peace. I had peace *with* God as a result of Jesus' work on the cross. And I had the peace *of* God, that is, the inner witness of His Spirit that I now had eternal life.

This inner witness of the Spirit is highly personal. That is, the Spirit tailors His witness to our particular temperament and circumstances. Each of us comes to the point of trusting in Christ from different experiences—some from a flagrantly sinful life, others from a highly moral and even religious background. For the former, there may be a deep, penetrating assurance that his sins are forgiven, that he has been washed clean and has a new life in Christ. For the moral or religious person there may be a sense of relief that she no longer has to try to earn God's favor. For me, it was a quiet sense of peace; my five-year struggle with God was over. In every case, though, it is the Spirit's application of the gospel to our lives that produces this inner witness.

We need this inner witness of the Spirit, not only at the time we come to Christ, but throughout our Christian lives, especially in times of severe temptation and failure. Once I was on my way to speak at a conference on the pursuit of holiness. The trip itself had been one of those stressful experiences when I did not exhibit the fruit of the Spirit of love, joy, and peace to airline personnel. I felt like an utter failure (which was true). How could I possibly speak to others about pursuing holiness when I had been so unholy myself?

Arriving at my hotel room late at night, I opened my Bible to try to find some encouragement. Soon I came to a short phrase in Colossians 2:13: "He forgave us all our sins." My heart was flooded with joy. The Spirit bore witness with my spirit that my sins of that very day were forgiven, washed away by the blood of Christ. I was emboldened with courage to speak at that conference, not because I was good enough, but because the Holy Spirit bore witness with my spirit that my sins were forgiven.

THE WORK OF THE SPIRIT

At the beginning of this chapter, I referred to 1 John 5:13, where John said, "I write these things to you who believe in the name of the Son of God so that you may know that you have eternal life." Obviously John had given some indicators earlier in his letter for that purpose. In 1 John 5:10-12, John alludes to the first two means of assurance God has given us: belief in His testimony regarding His Son and the internal witness of the Spirit in our hearts.

However, John also adds two additional indicators that can be grouped under the category of the work of the Spirit in us. The first is found in 1 John 2:29: "If you know that he is righteous, you know that everyone who does what is right has been born of him." This test can be a tricky one because we may understand John to say that only those who *always* do what is right are born of God. Though that is certainly God's standard for us, it is obvious that none of us measures up to it. And even John himself says, "If we claim to be without sin, we deceive ourselves and the truth is not in us" (1 John 1:8).

The *New King James Version* and the *New American Standard*

Bible can help us understand what John means. Both translations say, "Everyone who *practices* righteousness is born of God." John, then, is not writing of sinlessness, of *always* doing what is right, but of our normal practice, of the dominant direction of our lives.

Sometimes our obedience is marked more by desire than by performance. So we have to ask ourselves: "Is my life characterized by an *earnest* desire and a *sincere* effort to obey God in all that He commands? What is my attitude toward God's Law? Do I find it to be holy, just, and good? And do I delight in it in my inner being even though I find my sinful nature struggling against it?" (See Romans 7:12,22-23.)

Accompanying our sincere desire to obey God will be a heightened sensitivity to our indwelling sin. Often it is our increased awareness of sin that causes us to doubt our salvation or to give Satan an inroad into our minds to suggest that "a Christian wouldn't sin like you do." But think about that accusation for a moment. Satan would certainly not suggest such a thought to an unbeliever. Rather, he wants unbelievers to be complacent about their sin. So turn the tables on Satan and your own internal doubts. Ask yourself if those accusations or doubts are not really a sign that you do trust Christ.

There is a story about Martin Luther, perhaps apocryphal, that in a dream he saw Satan standing before him with a long list of his sins. Luther supposedly asked, "Is that all of them?" to which Satan replied, "No, there are many more." Luther then said, "Put them all down and then write across the whole lot of them, 'The blood of Jesus Christ cleanses me from all sin.'" Whether this story is true or not, it teaches us how to deal with doubts caused by our sin. We are not to deny or minimize them. Instead we should take them to the cross and see Jesus bearing those sins for us. That very act will motivate us to deal with those sins that are causing our doubts.

DO WE LOVE EACH OTHER?

The second indicator John gives of the Holy Spirit's work in us is found in 1 John 3:14: "We know that we have passed from death to life, because we love our brothers." Do you love other believers? First of all, do you enjoy their company? Do you want to gather with them to worship God, or do you prefer to do other things?

I once became baffled while seeking to help another believer who was struggling with assurance. Nothing I suggested seemed to work. He continued to struggle. Then one day he told me his struggle was over. He had come across 1 John 3:14. As he thought about that verse, he said, "I do love my brothers. I do love other believers. I rejoice to be around them and fellowship with them. I must truly be a Christian." The Holy Spirit had used that Scripture and his own attitude toward other believers to give him assurance that he was indeed a child of God.

Love of our brothers and sisters, however, is more than just enjoying Christian fellowship with them. We should also ask ourselves if our love is the kind Paul described in 1 Corinthians 13:4-7. Are we patient, kind, gracious, slow to anger, and ready to forgive? Again, none of us can completely measure up to such a standard, but do you want to? Do you grieve over your failures in those areas? If so, you love your brothers.

Of course, these two indicators cut both ways. Paul wrote to the Corinthians, "Examine yourselves to see whether you are in the faith; test yourselves. Do you not realize that Christ Jesus is in you—unless, of course, you fail the test?" (2 Corinthians 13:5).

We should never be afraid to examine ourselves. But when doubts do arise, the solution is not to try harder to prove to ourselves that we are believers. The solution is to flee to the cross and to the righteousness of Christ, which is our only hope. And then, having looked to Christ alone for our justification, we can look to His Spirit to enable us to deal with those areas of our lives that cause doubt.

The work of the Spirit within us is as much a gift of God's grace as is our justification and adoption as sons. But whereas justification and adoption are instantaneous and complete at once, our growth in Christlikeness is a lifelong process. Therefore, we should never look solely to our love and obedience for our assurance of salvation. At most they can demonstrate our salvation, never prove it. Ultimately our assurance must rest on the gospel and on the fact that God has said that all who call on the name of the Lord shall be saved.

The unsearchable riches of Christ are a treasure trove of blessings given to us. Part of that treasure is the assurance God gives that we do have eternal life. Don't stop short of availing yourself of His riches until you have that assurance.

CHAPTER FOURTEEN

WE SHALL BE LIKE HIM

—⟨≈≈⟩—

In chapter 12 we saw the apostle John's astonishing statement that we (that is, all believers) are children of God. We explored what that means for us in this life as those who have been both born of God and adopted as sons of God. But the good news doesn't stop there. John continues on in 1 John 3:2: "Dear friends, now we are children of God, and what we will be has not yet been made known. But we know that when he appears, we shall be like him, for we shall see him as he is."

For John, there is both a glorious present (now we are children of God) and an even more glorious future—when He appears we shall be like Him. To be like Jesus is the hope we can look forward to. In fact, the apostle Paul wrote that we have been predestined by God to be conformed to the likeness of His Son (see Romans 8:29). Likeness to Christ, then, is God's ultimate purpose for us and the hope we look forward to. What does it mean to be like Jesus?

LIKE HIM IN SPIRIT

First, it means to be like Him in spirit; that is, in our true inner being. This is a process that begins at conversion and will reach its ultimate fulfillment when we enter the Lord's presence at death. Paul calls this process *transformation*. "But we all, with unveiled face, beholding as in a mirror the glory of the Lord, are being *transformed* into the same image from glory to glory, just as from the Lord, the Spirit" (2 Corinthians 3:18, NASB, emphasis added).[1] So God has predestined us to be conformed to the likeness or image of His Son, and He is now at work in us through His Spirit to bring that to pass.

Meanwhile, however, we find that we still struggle with the remains of indwelling sin. "For the sinful nature desires what is contrary to the Spirit, and the Spirit what is contrary to the sinful nature. They are in conflict with each other, so that you do not do what you want" (Galatians 5:17). A continuous internal conflict wages between two opposing forces in our hearts. We find that when we want to do good, evil is right there with us (see Romans 7:21). We continue to struggle with pride, selfishness, impatience, a critical spirit, a sharp tongue, a lack of love, and countless expressions of our sinful natures. Even though the Spirit is at work in us and is transforming us, our sinful nature opposes Him every step of the way.

We will have this struggle as long as we live in these bodies. It is painful because we are at war within ourselves, and continually we have to say no to sinful desires. It is sometimes humiliating as sinful traits reveal themselves to our consciousness. Or perhaps we have, so to speak, soared into the heavenlies with Christ in our morning devotions, only to come crashing down with a thud before nine o'clock through some conflict with another person.

We long to be released from this warfare, and one day we will be. Hebrews 12:22-24 gives us a quick preview of heaven as it is now, and in that passage we read of "the spirits of righteous men made perfect" (verse 23). This is a reference to the believers of all ages whose spirits are now with Christ in heaven. The writer of Hebrews says they are now "made perfect." This means the sinful nature that now clings to our spirits like dirty, wet clothes will be completely done away with, and our spirits will be completely conformed to the likeness of Christ. This happens immediately at death when we go directly into the presence of the Lord.

The period between our death and the still-future resurrection of our bodies is usually called the *intermediate state*. The Bible actually tells us little about this period, but what it does say is very encouraging. In 2 Corinthians 5:8 Paul says that he "would prefer to be away from the body and at home with the Lord," and in Philippians 1:23 he says, "I desire to depart and be with Christ, which is better by far." Taking Paul's statements along with Hebrews 12:22-24, we can say that in the intermediate state:

- We will be with Christ.
- We will be in the presence of thousands upon thousands of angels in joyful assembly. (Will we perhaps still hear those seraphs of Isaiah 6:1-3 calling out antiphonally, "Holy, holy, holy is the Lord Almighty"?)
- We will be with all believers of all ages.
- We will be perfectly conformed to Christ in our spirits.
- We will be in a state that is "far better" than anything we can imagine.

It is difficult for us to visualize an existence in heaven without the benefit of our physical senses; or, for that matter, a physical brain. Yet we need to remember that God has existed eternally without a physical body. And even the angels apparently exist only in spirit (though some have assumed a physical body at times for specific purposes). Though we cannot understand *how* these things will be, we need to submit our minds to the teaching of Scripture and look forward to the time when we also will be with Christ, when our spirits will be made perfect, and when we will be in a state that is "far better" than our best conditions on earth.

OUR HOMECOMING

What will it be like when we enter the presence of the Lord? Sometimes when I focus too much on my own shortcomings, of how often I have sinned against grace and against knowledge, of how little I have availed myself of all the blessings of God and opportunities that have come my way, I think that I would like to somehow "just slip in the side door" of heaven, unnoticed and consequently unwelcomed. But that is because I *do* focus too much on myself and try to anticipate my welcome on the basis of my performance.

The apostle Peter, however, gives us an entirely different perspective in 2 Peter 1:10-11: "Therefore, my brothers, be all the more eager to make your calling and election sure. For if you do these things, you will never fall, and you will receive a rich welcome into the eternal kingdom of our Lord and Savior Jesus Christ."

Note especially verse 11: "and you will receive a *rich welcome* into the eternal kingdom of our Lord and Savior Jesus Christ" (emphasis added). This is a picture of a grand and glorious homecoming. At the end of World War II thousands of servicemen returned home from Europe and the Far East. As the various ships on which they returned arrived in ports here in the United States, they were greeted by cheering crowds and lively bands. And if relatives were able to be present, there was the added excitement of tearful hugs and joyful kisses. These servicemen received a *rich welcome* back home.

This is the way it will be with us, only on a much grander scale. If we have, to use Peter's words, made our calling and election sure, we will receive a rich welcome into Christ's eternal kingdom. It might appear, upon a casual reading of this Scripture, that our rich welcome is indeed dependent on our doing "these things" (that is, the "doings" of verses 5 through 7). However, the doing of these things—that is, pursuing the particular Christian virtues mentioned in verses 5 through 7—is not the basis of the rich welcome. Rather, it is the means (or one of the means—see chapter 13) whereby we make our calling and election sure. In other words, it is a way we assure ourselves that we have been made new creations in Christ (see 2 Corinthians 5:17) and do have the hope of eternal life.

There will be no slipping in the side door of heaven with our head hanging down and, to use a popular idiom, our tail between our legs. No, no, a thousand times no! Everyone who has been the object of God's calling and election will receive a rich welcome into Christ's eternal kingdom, not because we deserve it, but because we have been clothed with the spotless robe of Christ's righteousness. It will be because we are united to Him who is the object of the Father's everlasting love and delight that we also will be received as objects of His love and delight.

There is a somewhat obscure verse in the Psalms (116:15) that gives us God's perspective on our entrance into His eternal kingdom:

Precious in the sight of the Lord
is the death of his saints.

Why is this true? We think of death as a parting. We think of "losing a loved one" through death. But from God's perspective, the death of a believer is just the opposite. It is a homecoming. It is precious in His sight.

Think of the relatives awaiting the arrival of the ship carrying their returning husbands, fathers, and sons from the war. See the ship steaming into the harbor with servicemen lining the rails. Look at the expressions of joy and anticipation on the faces of those relatives as they eagerly await the docking of the ship and the setting up of the gangplank. The return of those men is precious in the sight of their loved ones. And this is just a pale picture of how God anticipates the arrival "home" of His sons and daughters from our own spiritual war of this life.

LIKE HIM IN BODY

As glorious as will be our "homecoming" at death, there will be an even more glorious time at the resurrection when our perfected spirits are united with our resurrection bodies. It is this ultimate hope to which John refers in 1 John 3:2: "But we know that when he appears, we shall be like him, for we shall see him as he is." At the resurrection we shall be like Jesus, not only in spirit, but also in body.

Paul writes of the same reality in Philippians 3:20-21: "But our citizenship is in heaven. And we eagerly await a Savior from there, the Lord Jesus Christ, who, by the power that enables him to bring everything under his control, will transform our lowly bodies so that they will be like his glorious body." Note the contrast Paul draws between our present *lowly* bodies and our future bodies that will be like His *glorious* body.

In this present life our bodies are subject to suffering, sickness, disabilities, decay, ugliness, aging, and finally death. It is not a pretty picture. One has only to go to an event such as a twenty-fifth high school class reunion to realize that soon after reaching full adulthood, our bodies begin to deteriorate. We joke about it at such occasions, but the fact is that in this life, because of the curse of sin, our bodies are lowly bodies.

That is why Paul also wrote, "But we ourselves, who have the firstfruits of the Spirit, groan inwardly as we wait eagerly for our adoption as sons, the redemption of our bodies" (Romans 8:23). We groan. Between the internal conflict with our sinful nature and the external struggles with our lowly bodies, as well as the frustrations of adverse circumstances that so frequently beset us, we groan. But this groaning is not without purpose. Instead it causes us, or should cause us, to wait *eagerly* for the redemption of our bodies. Paul says it is in this hope that we are saved (see Romans 8:24). God intends that the struggles of this life wean us from our attachments to this present world. Generally speaking, believers who have the least benefits of this life have the most vigorous hopes of heaven.

Note that in Romans 8:23 Paul speaks of our *adoption as sons*, the redemption of our bodies. We saw in chapter 12 that we have already been adopted into God's family (see Romans 8:15, "but you received the Spirit of sonship"). But here in verse 23, just a few sentences later, Paul speaks of adoption as a future prospect. Adoption, therefore, is both a present privilege and a final blessing to be confirmed at the resurrection. Some commentators say that the Romans practiced a twofold adoption—one private, the other public—and that Paul had in mind this two-stage adoption in verses 15 and 23. Whether that is true or not, Paul certainly uses the word *adoption* in a twofold sense, denoting a present reality and a future hope. So, although our adoption is complete and absolutely irrevocable the moment we trust in Christ, the full manifestation of it awaits the redemption of our bodies at the resurrection, when our lowly bodies will be made like His glorious body.

WHAT WILL IT BE LIKE?

Just as it is difficult for us to visualize our existence in the intermediate state, so it is difficult for us to know what Paul and John mean by our being like Christ in His glorious body. On this subject, we do well to stick to the wording of Scripture. Here, then, are the words of Paul and John:

- "So will it be with the resurrection of the dead. The body that is sown is perishable, it is raised imperishable; it is sown in dishonor, it is raised in glory; it is sown in weakness, it is raised in power; it is sown a natural body, it is raised a spiritual body. If there is a natural body, there is also a spiritual body" (1 Corinthians 15:42-44).
- "Listen, I tell you a mystery: We will not all sleep, but we will all be changed—in a flash, in the twinkling of an eye, at the last trumpet. For the trumpet will sound, the dead will be raised imperishable, and we will be changed. For the perishable must clothe itself with the imperishable, and the mortal with immortality. When the perishable has been clothed with the imperishable, and the mortal with immortality, then the saying that is written will come true: 'Death has been swallowed up in victory'" (1 Corinthians 15:51-54).
- "And I heard a loud voice from the throne saying, 'Now the dwelling of God is with men, and he will live with them. They will be his people, and God himself will be

with them and be their God. He will wipe every tear from their eyes. There will be no more death or mourning or crying or pain, for the old order of things has passed away'" (Revelation 21:3-4).

- "No longer will there be any curse. The throne of God and of the Lamb will be in the city, and his servants will serve him. They will see his face, and his name will be on their foreheads. There will be no more night. They will not need the light of a lamp or the light of the sun, for the Lord God will give them light. And they will reign for ever and ever" (Revelation 22:3-5).

Note that Paul emphasizes the strong difference between the natural, mortal body and the spiritual, immortal body. But both are *bodies*. Our perfected spirits will be at home in our immortal bodies. What exactly this spiritual body looks like or how it functions, we do not know. We only know it will be like the Lord's glorious body, and in that we put our hope and expectations.

In the Revelation passages the apostle John emphasizes a different aspect of our resurrection life. While Paul, at least in 1 Corinthians 15, emphasizes the reality of an immortal, spiritual body, John calls our attention to the reality of our eternal presence with God: "Now the dwelling of God is with men, and he will live with them" (21:3) and "The throne of God and of the Lamb will be in the city, and his servants will serve him. They will see his face" (22:3-4).

Believers who have passed on from this life are now with the Lord and are perfected in their spirits. If Christ does not return first, all of us who are now reading these words will one day join them. But the day will come when our perfected spirits and immortal bodies are forever united. And in that glorious condition "we will be with the Lord forever"

(1 Thessalonians 4:17). Hallelujah! At that time we will experience the full reality of the unsearchable riches of Christ.

But before we experience that glorious reality, we still live in this life. During our sojourn here we are not just to wait for our hope of heaven, but are to be actively and vigorously engaged in becoming more like Christ (a process usually called *sanctification*) and of extending the rule of His kingdom (the first three petitions of the Lord's Prayer in Matthew 6:9-13). To these two ends we will devote the final chapters of this book.

CHAPTER FIFTEEN

THE GOSPEL AND SANCTIFICATION

"What shall we say, then? Shall we go on sinning so that grace may increase?" the apostle Paul asks in Romans 6:1. If we are justified freely by God's grace through the work of Christ, doesn't more sin increasingly magnify God's grace?

"Certainly not!" responds Paul, "How shall we who died to sin live any longer in it?" (Romans 6:2, NKJV). Paul's response is not an impatient "How could you think such a thing?" Rather, as he demonstrates in the following verses, such a practice cannot occur because a fundamental change has occurred in our relationship to sin. The expression Paul uses for this decisive change is, "We died to sin."

DEAD TO SIN

Now here is the difficult part. What does Paul mean when he says that we died to sin? It's fairly obvious he does not mean that we died to the daily committal of sin. If that were true, no honest person could claim to be justified, because we all sin daily (as we saw in chapter 2). Nor does it mean that we died in the sense of being no longer responsive to sin's temptations. If that were true, Peter's admonition to abstain from sinful desires (see 1 Peter 2:11) would be pointless. So what does Paul mean?

Conservative evangelical commentators have generally taken one of two positions in answering this question.

Several have held that Paul refers exclusively to the *guilt* of sin. That is, through our union with Christ in His death, we died to sin's guilt. This view would seem to be consistent with Paul's statement in Romans 7:4 that through Christ we died to the Law; not to the law as an expression of God's moral will, but to the condemnation and curse of the Law. To say we died to the *guilt* of sin and to the *condemnation* of the Law addresses the same issue.

Other commentators say that Paul means we died to the *reign* and *dominion* of sin in our lives. In other words, because sin no longer exercises absolute dominion over us, we no longer *can* (speaking of ability) continue in sin as a predominant way of life. We struggle with sin, and we do sin, but sin no longer is our master. In the opinion of these commentators, this is the only view that addresses Paul's question, "Shall we go on sinning so that grace may increase?"

I believe both views should be brought together. *The guilt of our sin in Adam resulted in our being given over to sin's dominion as a penal consequence.* When a judge sentences a person convicted of a crime to five years in prison, that sentence is the penal consequence of the crime. That is analogous to what God did to Adam and all his posterity. Part of the penal consequence of Adam's sin was to be delivered over to the dominion or bondage of sin. That is why David said, "Surely I was sinful at birth, sinful from the time my mother conceived me" (Psalm 51:5). We have already looked at Paul's description of this bondage in Ephesians 2:1-3 (see chapter 11).

In the case of the prisoner who has served his five years, his penal consequences are over. The broken law no longer has a claim against him. In that sense he has ended his relationship to the law and its penal consequences. He must continue to obey the law in the future, but the particular offense that sent him to prison has been dealt with forever. To use Paul's expression, he has died to the law and its penal consequences.

How does this apply to us? Let me paraphrase from the comments of John Brown, a nineteenth-century Scottish pastor, theologian, and author of several commentaries:

> The wages of sin is death. Until the condemning sentence is executed, a person is subject to sin, both in its power to condemn and its power to deprave [or exert dominion]. But let the penal consequences be fully endured, let the law's penalty be fully paid, and the person is at once delivered from sin's condemning power and its depraving influence or dominion. It is in this way that all that are in Christ Jesus, all that have been justified by His grace, have died, not in their own persons, but in the person of their Surety. They are therefore delivered from the reign of sin— from its power to condemn, and therefore, also from its power to rule in the heart and life.[1]

To say it again, our slavery to the dominion of sin was the result of our guilt incurred by Adam's sin, further aggravated by our own personal sin. Through our union with Christ in His death, however, our guilt, both from Adam's and from our own sins, was forever dealt with. Having then died with Christ to the guilt of sin, we died to, or were delivered from, the dominion of sin. Whether we say we died to the dominion of sin, or we were delivered from the dominion of sin through our death to the guilt of sin, the result is the same. We no longer continue in sin as a dominant lifestyle. Sin no longer has dominion over us.

DEFINITIVE SANCTIFICATION

This death to, or deliverance from, the dominion of sin is often called *definitive sanctification.* You are probably more or less familiar with the word *sanctification,* which historically has been used as a shorthand expression for Christian growth. Its basic meaning, however, is "separation," and in using the term *definitive sanctification* we are speaking of a decisive break with, or separation from, sin as a ruling power in the believer's life. It is a point-in-time event occurring simultaneously with justification. It is a change wrought in us by the monergistic action of the Holy Spirit as He removes us from the kingdom of darkness and brings us into the kingdom of Christ (see Colossians 1:13). That is why Paul could write to the Corinthian believers as those who had already been sanctified, even though they were still quite immature in their Christian walk (1 Corinthians 1:2,30; 6:11). This definitive break with the dominion of sin, which is solely the work of the Holy Spirit, occurs in the life of everyone who trusts in Christ as Savior. There is no such thing as justification without definitive sanctification.

COUNT YOURSELVES DEAD TO SIN

So we are free from both the guilt and the reigning power or dominion of sin in our lives. Of what use is this information to us? How can it help us when we are struggling with some persistent sin pattern and see ourselves often giving in to our sinful desires? Here is where Paul's instructions in Romans 6:11 can help us: "In the same way, count yourselves dead to sin but alive to God in Christ Jesus."

It is important that we understand Paul's point, because he is not telling is to *do* something but to *believe* something. We are to count on, or believe, that we are dead to sin. First of all, we are dead to its guilt. God no longer counts it against us. We are no longer under condemnation because of it (see Romans 4:8; 8:1).

This is not make-believe. You are indeed guilty in yourself, but God no longer regards you as guilty, because the guilt of your sin has already been borne by Christ as your substitute. The sentence has been served. The penalty has been paid. To use Paul's expression, you have died to sin's guilt.

I know that when we are painfully conscious of sin in our lives, it is difficult to count on the fact that we are dead to its guilt. All the more reason to hold steadfast to the promise of God. Just as it seemed incredible to Abraham that he could have a son when he was nearly a hundred years old and Sarah's womb was dead, so it often seems incredible to us to believe that we have died to sin's guilt when it appears so ugly in our own sight. But just as Abraham did not weaken in faith, but believed the promise of God, so we must believe what God says to us. There is *no* condemnation for those who are in Christ Jesus. We have died to sin's guilt.

William Romaine (born 1714) was one of the leaders of the eighteenth-century revival in England, along with George Whitefield and the Wesley brothers. In his classic work on faith he wrote, "No sin can be crucified either in heart or life, unless it be first pardoned in conscience, because there will be want of faith to receive the strength of Jesus, by whom alone it can be crucified. If it be not mortified in its guilt, it cannot be subdued in its power."[2]

What Romaine was saying is that if you do not believe you are dead to sin's guilt, you cannot trust Christ for the strength to subdue its power in your life. So the place to begin in dealing with sin in your life is to count on the fact that you died to its guilt through your union with Christ in His death. This is an important truth you need to ponder and pray over until the Holy Spirit convinces you of it in both your head and heart.

DO NOT LET SIN REIGN

We have, however, died not only to sin's guilt but also to its reigning power in our lives. Here sin is viewed as an active principle that seeks to dominate us. As an analogy to help us understand, the will to live is an active principle within us. With few exceptions, that principle always asserts itself when we are faced with a life-threatening situation. We instinctively fight to save our lives.

Now, although sin as an active principle is still with us, it can no longer reign supreme in our lives. We are united to Christ, and His Holy Spirit has come to reside in us. We have been delivered from the power of Satan and given a new heart (see Ezekiel 36:26; Acts 26:18). However, as believers we do experience the tension Paul describes in Galatians 5:17: "For the sinful nature desires what is contrary to the Spirit, and the Spirit what is contrary to the sinful nature. They are in conflict with each other, so that you do not do what you want."

George Smeaton described the tension this way:

> There [is] an internal conflict between flesh and spirit—between an old and new nature. And the strange thing is, that in this conflict the power and

faculties of the Christian seem to be occupied at one time by the one, and at another time by the other. The same intellect, will, and affections come under different influences, like two conflicting armies occupying the ground, and in turn driven from the field.[3]

Another way of describing this tension between the sinful nature and the Spirit is to liken it to a tug-of-war. With two opposing teams pulling on the rope, its direction of movement often goes back and forth until one team eventually prevails. This is the way it will be with us until the Holy Spirit finally prevails.

We must acknowledge this tension if we are to make progress in the Christian life. Indwelling sin is like a disease that we can't begin to deal with until we acknowledge its presence. But in the case of sin, we must also count on the fact that, though it still resides in us, it no longer has dominion over us. As Paul said, "For sin shall not be your master, because you are not under law, but under grace" (Romans 6:14).

Therefore, because we have the assurance that sin shall not be our master, we are not to let it reign in our mortal bodies so that we obey its evil desires (see Romans 6:12). Rather we are, by the enabling power of the Spirit, to put to death the misdeeds of the body (Romans 8:13), and to abstain from sinful desires, which war against our souls (1 Peter 2:11). Indeed, we are called to an active, vigorous warfare against the principle of sin that remains in us.

CHRIST'S POWER, NOT OURS

However, we are not to wage this warfare in the strength of our own willpower. Instead, just as we by faith look to Christ for our righteous standing before God, so by faith we are to look to

Him for the enabling power to live the Christian life. This power comes to us as a result of our vital or living union with Him. Jesus referred to this union in John 15:1-5 when He called Himself the vine and us the branches. Through that metaphor He was teaching us that just as the branches derive their life and nourishment from the vine, so we are to receive our spiritual life and power from Him.

All believers are spiritually united to Christ in such a way that our spiritual life comes from Him. We are not completely passive, however, in this relationship. Rather we are to abide or remain in Him by faith. That is, we are to *actively* rely on Christ for the enabling power we need to wage war against the sin that remains in us, to put on the positive virtues of Christlike character (called the *fruit of the Spirit* in Galatians 5:22-23), and to serve Christ effectively in all that He calls us to do.

The apostle Paul had in mind our union with Christ and the power that comes from Him in such Scriptures as Philippians 4:13, "I can do everything through him who gives me strength;" and Colossians 1:29, "To this end I labor, struggling with all his energy, which so powerfully works in me." Paul waged war against indwelling sin, and he worked hard in ministry, but he did both in dependence on Christ and the power that comes through a living union with Him.

PROGRESSIVE SANCTIFICATION

Warring against the sin that remains in us and putting on Christlike character is usually called *sanctification*. But because the term *definitive sanctification* is used to describe the point-in-time decisive deliverance from the dominion of sin, it is helpful to speak of Christian growth as *progressive sanctification*. The word *progressive* indicates growth or positive change. To return to the tug-of-war analogy, it assumes that, though the rope may move back and forth, over time it moves in the right direction until finally we win the tug-of-war against sin at the end of our lives.

There is no doubt that the tug-of-war rope must move in the right direction. The New Testament writers both assume growth and continually urge us to pursue it. We are to pursue holiness "more and more," and to love each other "more and more" (1 Thessalonians 4:1,9-10). We are to possess the qualities of Christian character "in increasing measure" (2 Peter 1:8). However, we can always expect resistance. To stay with the tug-of-war analogy, although the Spirit who dwells within us is stronger than the sinful nature, that nature continues to "dig in its heels" every step of the way. And sometimes it will pull the rope in the wrong direction.

What is it then that will keep us going in the face of this internal conflict? The answer is: the gospel. It is the assurance in the gospel that we have indeed died to the guilt of sin; that there is no condemnation for us who are in Christ Jesus; that the Lord will never count our sins against us; and that we are truly delivered from the reigning power of sin, that will motivate us and keep us going even in the midst of the tension between the Spirit and the sinful nature.

We must always keep focused on the gospel. Horatius Bonar, another nineteenth-century Scottish pastor and author, wrote:

> The secret of a believer's holy walk is his continual
> recurrence to the blood of the Surety, and his daily
> [communion] with a crucified and risen Lord. All
> divine life, and all precious fruits of it, pardon, peace,
> and holiness, spring from the cross. All fancied sanctifi-
> cation which does not arise wholly from the blood of

the cross is nothing better than Pharisaism. If we would be holy, we must get to the cross, and dwell there; else, notwithstanding all our labour, diligence, fasting, praying and good works, we shall be yet void of real sanctification, destitute of those humble, gracious tempers which accompany a clear view of the cross.

False ideas of holiness are common, not only among those who profess false religions, but among those who profess the true. The love of God to us, and our love to Him, work together for producing holiness. Terror accomplishes no real obedience. Suspense brings forth no fruit unto holiness. No gloomy uncertainty as to God's favour can subdue one lust, or correct our crookedness of will. But the free pardon of the cross uproots sin, and withers all its branches. Only the certainty of love, forgiving love, can do this. . . .

Free and warm reception into the divine favour is the strongest of all motives in leading a man to seek conformity to Him who has thus freely forgiven him all trespasses.[4]

Paul said the same thing very succinctly when he wrote, "For Christ's love compels us" (2 Corinthians 5:14). To be compelled is to be highly motivated. That is, we are to be motivated by Christ's love for us. And where do we learn of His love? Where do we hear Him say, "I love you"? It is in the gospel. The gospel, received in our hearts at salvation, guarantees definitive sanctification. And the gospel believed every day is the only enduring motivation to pursue progressive sanctification. That is why we need to "preach the gospel to ourselves every day." It is in the gospel that we find those unsearchable riches of Christ that produce not only justification but also sanctification.[5]

CHAPTER SIXTEEN

TO THE ENDS OF THE EARTH

In 1784 a group of ministers in the midlands of England sent out an urgent request for prayer to all of their constituent churches. They requested prayer for revival in their own and other churches of England, and for "the spread of the gospel to the most distant parts of the habitable globe."[1]

To us in the twenty-first century, a call to prayer for world evangelism does not seem unusual. But we have an advantage these men knew nothing about. Today we can survey the results of over two hundred years of missionary activity beginning with William Carey's venture to India in 1793. But in 1784 not one of those ministers had ever met a missionary.[2]

The question then arises: If these pastors had never met a missionary, had never attended a missions conference, had never read a missionary prayer letter, where did their sense of urgency originate? The answer is from the Bible, specifically those passages of Scripture that teach us about God's plan for the spread of the gospel to the whole world.

In this book we have been exploring what the apostle Paul called "the unsearchable riches of Christ" (Ephesians 3:8); that is, the gospel. We have examined our need of the gospel, the work of Christ in meeting our need, and the application of His work to our individual lives in justification, adoption, glorification, and sanctification. If we stopped at this point, it could seem as if the gospel promotes only an attitude of pure self-interest on our part: What will the gospel do for me? Or at most, the gospel would be about God and me. But the gospel is not about God and me. The gospel is about God and the world. It is about God who "was in Christ reconciling the world to Himself" (2 Corinthians 5:19, NKJV).

We are not to be a terminus point for the gospel, but rather a way station in its progress to the ends of the earth. God intends that everyone who has embraced the gospel become a part of the great enterprise of spreading the gospel. What our particular part in this great enterprise may be will vary from person to person, but all of us should be involved. It is not my intent in this chapter to explore what your role might be. Rather, I want to explore some of the Scriptures likely used to motivate those eighteenth-century ministers to issue a call for prayer for world missions, because it is those same Scriptures that should motivate us today.

ALL NATIONS WILL BE BLESSED

A good starting point is Genesis 12:3, where God promises Abraham that "all peoples on earth will be blessed through you." God repeats this promise in Genesis 22:18, where He more specifically says, "through your offspring all nations on earth will be blessed." In Galatians 3:16 the apostle Paul identifies this "off-spring" as Christ. God's promise to Abraham, then, is that all nations will be blessed through Christ—that is, through His atoning work for us. This theme of all the nations being blessed through Christ continues throughout the Old Testament. Here are just two passages of Scripture that represent many more:

- "May his name endure forever; may it continue as long as the sun. All nations will be blessed through him, and they will call him blessed" (Psalm 72:17).
- "He says: 'It is too small a thing for you to be my servant to restore the tribes of Jacob and bring back those of Israel I have kept. I will also make you a light for the Gentiles, that you may bring my salvation to the ends of the earth'" (Isaiah 49:6).

THE REIGN OF CHRIST

There is, however, a parallel theme running through the Old Testament regarding the worldwide reign of Christ. A primary passage on this theme is Psalm 22:27-28:

> All the ends of the earth
> will remember and turn to the LORD,
> and all the families of the nations
> will bow down before him,
> for dominion belongs to the LORD
> and he rules over the nations.

This concept of the universal reign of Christ is again traceable through the remainder of the Old Testament, but is stated most explicitly in Matthew 28:18-20, the passage commonly called *the Great Commission:*

> Then Jesus came to them and said, "All authority in heaven and on earth has been given to me. Therefore go and make disciples of all nations, baptizing them in the name of the Father and of the Son and of the Holy

Spirit, and teaching them to obey everything I have commanded you. And surely I am with you always, to the very end of the age."

Jesus begins His Great Commission by asserting that all authority in heaven and on earth has been given to Him. In view of this, He commands His disciples to go and make disciples of all nations. In the specific context, then, the command to make disciples means to bring people of all nations under the sway of Christ's authority. Whatever other meanings we may include in the word *disciple,* it must capture this idea of coming under the reign and rule of Jesus Christ.

So we see that there are two parallel goals: the blessing of Christ to all nations and the reign of Christ among all nations. The first of these goals focuses on the need of people. People need to be saved. People need to be rescued from the wrath of God that is surely coming. People need to be redeemed from their futile, destructive, and empty ways of life. The blessing to all nations addresses the desperate need of people in those nations to hear and embrace the gospel, to trust in Jesus Christ as their Savior.

The second goal focuses on the reign of Jesus Christ in the hearts of those people. Jesus came to save them so that He might reign in their lives. He came "to redeem us from all wickedness and to purify for himself a people that are his very own, eager to do what is good" (Titus 2:14). This speaks of the rule and reign of Christ in the heart of every individual believer.

Now here is an important point. Both of these goals—the blessing to people and the reign of Jesus Christ—are accomplished through the successful proclamation of the gospel among all nations, or to the ends of the earth. As people believe the gospel and are saved, the reign of Christ, in principle, is established in their hearts. They are delivered from the dominion or kingdom of darkness and are brought into the kingdom of Christ (see Colossians 1:13). And it is God's will that this process should be carried out among all nations, even to the ends of the earth.

This, then, is our task: the proclamation of the gospel in all nations so that people of those nations will trust in Christ and be brought under His authority in their lives. We cannot quantify, in terms of numbers of people, what it means for a nation to be blessed, nor what is meant by "all the families of the nations will bow down before him," but surely these expressions signify more than just a token few from each nation. Surely they promise a significant penetration of the gospel among every nation, tribe, people, and language.

In fact, Revelation 7:9 seems to imply such a noteworthy result: "After this I looked and there before me was a great multitude that no one could count, from every nation, tribe, people and language, standing before the throne and in front of the Lamb. They were wearing white robes and were holding palm branches in their hands."

As we think today of the vast numbers of people still living in spiritual darkness, primarily in the so-called *10-40 window* (northern Africa, the Middle East, and southern Asia), we acknowledge that there is yet much spiritual ground to be possessed. We find ourselves in a situation similar to the Israelites in their conquest of Canaan. Immediately after recounting their defeat of thirty-one Canaanite kings, God said to Joshua, "There are still very large areas of land to be taken over" (Joshua 12:24–13:1). While we rejoice in the progress of the gospel in many parts of the world, we acknowledge that there is more work to do before we can say that every nation has been blessed.

When Jesus commissioned us to make disciples of all nations, He clearly intended that we meet this objective. Furthermore, He has the power to ensure that we do. He is not like a helpless football coach standing on the sidelines watching his vastly inferior team take a sound beating. To continue the football metaphor, while we don't know the final score, we do know that Jesus' "team" will eventually win. God will not be defeated by the powers of darkness.

OUR RESPONSE

If all this is true, if God has promised that all nations will be blessed and that all the ends of the earth will remember and turn to the Lord, how should we respond? I maintain that our response should begin with prayer. We should boldly and persistently plead in prayer the promises of God.

Daniel, one of the great men of the Bible, is our example. He lived during the Babylonian captivity of Judah. Toward the end of that foreign incarceration he understood, from reading Jeremiah 29:10, that the captivity would last seventy years. So he took God at His word and began to pray that He would fulfill His promise to restore the Jews to their home (see Daniel 9:1-19). He pleaded the promise of God. This is what we should do in response to God's promises of the success of the gospel. We should earnestly pray over such Scriptures as Genesis 22:18 and Psalm 22:27-28, asking God to fulfill His promises.

I am dismayed at how little we Christians pray for the success of the gospel among the nations. If we honestly examine our prayers, we find that we give the greatest priority to our own earthly needs. We pray about health needs, financial needs, weather needs, and all other kinds of needs of this life. Perhaps we even pray about our own or our loved ones' spiritual needs. But how many are praying about the spread of the gospel to the ends of the earth? How many are pleading the promises of God?

As a personal application of this challenge, I keep with my morning devotional material a small world map. Using that map I try to pray "around the world" over the course of a week. I put my finger on specific countries, especially those more resistant to Christianity, and ask God to bless those nations with a significant penetration of the gospel, so that His name will be glorified among them.

Consider the prayer Jesus taught us (see Matthew 6:9-13). While I do not think He intended that we always use the exact words He gave us, it seems evident He intended it as an example to be followed. This being true, then, we should notice the sequence of the requests. The first three requests are that His name be hallowed, His kingdom come, and His will be done. There is a certain degree of overlap in these three requests. God's name will be hallowed as His kingdom comes in the hearts of people. God's will will be done as people acknowledge the kingship of Christ in their lives and in their societies. All of these requests will be answered through the successful advance of the gospel to the ends of the earth.

In seeking to stimulate us to lift up our eyes to God's great objective for all nations, I do not intend to minimize the importance of evangelism and disciple-making at home. What I am seeking to do is to broaden our spiritual horizon; to get on our hearts what, according to Scripture, is on God's heart. I want us to realize that the gospel is not just about God and me, or even about God and the people among whom I live and work. The gospel is about God and the world.

Obviously, there is more to carrying out the Great Commission than prayer. People must go to the ends of the earth. As I write this chapter, our son, daughter-in-law, and one-year-old grandson are preparing to go to one of the more difficult areas of the 10-40 window. Is it hard to see them go to a people who are so resistant to the gospel? Absolutely! But if we are praying for the penetration of the gospel among those people, we must be prepared for God to use us or our loved ones to help answer those prayers.

Not only must people go, but we must provide financial support for them or for modern means of communication such as radio to reach places where people cannot go. Some of us must literally go, and all of us should participate in financial support. But the going is impotent and the financial support is futile if God does not go before us to open the eyes of the blind and turn them from darkness to light and from the power of Satan to God. And God does this as we plead His promises in prayer.

As we conclude, I pray that you have become more aware of the unsearchable riches of Christ that you possess through your union with Jesus Christ. I pray that you will realize the abundant riches of your inheritance in Christ and will not rest content with the spiritual equivalent of "fifty cents to buy a sack of cornmeal." And I pray just as fervently that you will be challenged to get on board with God's great plan to bless all nations, so that the ends of the earth will turn to the Lord.

The scope of the Great Commission is vast, and the obstacles to its fulfillment are formidable. But as we pray let us remember the words of Paul: "Now to him who is able to do immeasurably more than all we ask or imagine, according to his power that is at work within us, to him be glory in the church and in Christ Jesus throughout all generations, for ever and ever! Amen" (Ephesians 3:20-21). God is more than able. The Great Commission will be fulfilled. Will you be a part of it? Will you help others discover the unsearchable riches of Christ that you now enjoy?

THE GOSPEL FOR REAL LIFE
STUDY GUIDE

BY KAREN LEE-THORP

A Guide for Individual or Group Study

━━━∙∙∙━━━

If you would like to take a few weeks to let the ideas in this book sink from your head to your heart, this study guide is provided to help you. The ideal way to use it is to read two chapters of the book per week, write your thoughts about the questions in a notebook or journal, and then gather with a few friends to talk about what you found most significant. However, if you don't have time to write notes on the questions ahead of time, you can still gather with friends to discuss them. And if you aren't able to meet with a group, the Holy Spirit will not leave you as an orphan. He will be powerfully present as you read and write your thoughts.

You'll want a Bible handy to look up passages even though most of the passages are those discussed in the book. In this sense, the book has done a lot of the "Bible study" for you. Most of your discussion will revolve around these two questions: "Do I really understand this? Well enough that I could explain it to someone—including myself?" and "Do I really believe this? Not just theoretically, but deep down where my beliefs determine my feelings and actions?" Don't be afraid to use your feelings and actions as barometers of what your heart believes. It's normal to partly believe the gospel while we're on the way to fully believing it, and feelings and actions can help us spot the gaps.

STUDY 1

CHAPTERS 1 AND 2

1. If you're studying with a group, give each person one minute to share how he or she first became acquainted with the gospel. You won't have time to tell your whole testimony, but a brief snapshot will help you learn a lot about each other. (If you find this helpful, consider setting aside another meeting just to share testimonies. Or allow time at the beginning of each meeting for one or two people to tell a five-minute story of their journey to faith.)

2. Church historian Richard Lovelace writes, "below the surface of their lives [many Christians] are guilt-ridden and insecure . . . [and] draw the assurance of their acceptance with God from their sincerity, their past experience of conversion, their recent religious performance or the relative infrequency of their conscious, willful disobedience." Do you think that's true? If so, why do you think it's the case?

3. To what extent do you feel insecure about whether God loves or likes you?

4. What's wrong with a utilitarian view of the gospel that focuses on solutions to personal problems, a more successful life now, and assurance of going to heaven?

5. Read Romans 1:18; 3:10-12; Ephesians 2:3. Why does Bridges say it's so important to think about the bad news about ourselves: that we're by nature objects of God's wrath?

6. Read Matthew 18:21-35. How easy is it for you to imagine yourself as the servant who owed two hundred thousand years' wages to his master? Please explain why you feel that way.

7. Bridges says the primary need the gospel addresses is our need to be freed from the penalty and habitual practice of sin. On a typical day, how high does that need rate for you when compared to other concerns? Use a scale of 0 (not important to me at all) to 10 (the most important issue on my mind).

8. Read Romans 5:12-14. How did Adam's sin affect you?

9. Read Romans 5:15-19. How did Christ's death pay for your sin?

10. "Federal headship" perplexes many Christians. Does it seem fair to you that Adam's sin polluted you before you had a chance to do anything good or bad? Does it seem fair that Christ's death cleansed you from sin apart from anything you've done? Please explain.

11. Read the commandments and their definitions on pages 25-27. If this is the standard God has set for your life, how well do you measure up? Where are your main weaknesses?

12. Read Isaiah 6:1-7. When you imagine God's holiness, does it make you want to pull away from Him? Or does it make you want to approach Him fearlessly because Jesus' death on the cross has cleansed you? Please explain.

13. In light of what you've studied in chapters 1 and 2, what does "Jesus died for my sins" mean for you personally?

STUDY 2

CHAPTERS 3 AND 4

1. What pictures or feelings come to mind when you think of "obedience"?

2. Jesus could say, "I delight to do Your will, O my God" (Psalm 40:8, NASB). Why is it so important not just to want to do God's will but to *delight* in it?

3. In your own words, what was Jesus' "active obedience"? What did it do for you?

4. What was Jesus' "passive obedience"? What did it do for you?

5. A person gets legally united with Christ by placing faith— total reliance—in Him and His work. What difference does legal union with Christ make to your daily life (as opposed to what happens after you die)?

6. When God looks at you, He says, "This is my son [or daughter], whom I love; I am well pleased with him [or her]" not because of anything you've done, but because of what Christ did. What difference should that make to your daily life?

7. Bridges says, "God's justice must be satisfied; otherwise His moral government would be undermined" (page 43). Why would His moral government be undermined if He just forgave us without insisting that someone pay for our crimes?

8. Why does God treat your sins as seriously as He does rape and murder? Why doesn't He think you deserve more mercy than rapists and murderers?

9. To what extent (if at all) do you live in fear that God will punish you—or is punishing you—for your sins? What prompts you to fear or not fear this?

10. How will knowing that Christ has satisfied God's justice on your behalf affect the way you deal with:

   • an experience of suffering?

   • yourself when you sin?

   • an experience when someone else sins against you?

STUDY 3

CHAPTERS 5 AND 6

1. What pictures or feelings come to your mind when you think of "God's wrath"?

2. Read Matthew 5:22; Mark 9:47-48; Luke 12:4-7. How do you respond to this talk of hell and fearing God (and in the same breath Jesus' statement that you are worth more to God than the sparrows)?

3. How is God's wrath different from the wrath we may see humans display?

4. On pages 50-51, Bridges explains that God is wrathful against sin because sin is essentially an act of treason against the legitimate Ruler of the universe and His moral authority. Why is it inaccurate to see this wrathful God as an egotistical dictator?

5. Jesus *exhausted* God's wrath. The cup of wrath is empty. What are the implications of this fact for us?

6. What goes through your mind when you think about the fact that you "were the cause of our Savior's unimaginable suffering" as He took on God's wrath?

7. Why is it important for your current daily life to know that God has no more wrath when He looks at you?

8. Read Leviticus 16:20-22. How did Jesus do in reality what the live goat did symbolically in the ceremony on the Day of Atonement?

9. Bridges says (page 60), "Only to the extent we believe God has indeed put our sins behind His back will we be motivated and enabled to effectively deal with those sins in our daily lives." Why is this the case?

10. Which of the images of forgiveness discussed in chapter 6 (God putting your sins behind His back, remembering them no more, hurling them into the depths of the sea, and so on) speaks most deeply to you?

11. Why do you suppose it's so hard for many of us to shed our guilt feelings and believe that God has forgiven us?

12. Bridges counsels us to sincerely and humbly acknowledge our sins daily, and also to gratefully embrace God's forgiveness daily. How do you typically deal with sin in your life?

STUDY 4

CHAPTERS 7 AND 8

1. Read Galatians 3:10-14. Why were we under a curse from which we needed to be released?

2. Why isn't a little bit of disobedience something God can just accept without cursing us?

3. What would you say to someone who says, "I don't agree with all this talk of rules and obedience to the Law of God. The God I believe in isn't obsessed with rules like that."

4. In Romans 5:10, Paul writes that God hates sin and regards sinners as enemies. Why does simply wanting to live your own life your way make you an enemy of God? Why can't you be neutral toward God?

5. What would the world be like if God hated "big" sins like molesting children but not "ordinary" sins like wanting to run your own life? How would your life be different?

6. Read Ephesians 2:2-3. In what ways can you identify with the old life that Paul describes here?

7. How have you changed since "you were redeemed from the empty way of life handed down to you from your fore-fathers" (1 Peter 1:18)?

8. What should we do when our consciences accuse us of sins we still commit as Christians? See pages 79-80 and 1 John 1:5–2:2.

9. In light of what you've discussed so far, what does it mean to say that Jesus gave His life as a ransom for you?

10. In Romans 5:6, Paul says we were powerless to change our hearts to make them love God and His laws. So God did all that was necessary to reconcile us to Himself, including changing our hearts so we could respond in faith and gratitude. How do you respond to this?

11. As you think back over what you've read so far in this book, what picture of God emerges? What's He like? What's important to Him?

12. God has committed the message of reconciliation to us. Who helped you become reconciled to God? Whom have you helped?

STUDY 5

CHAPTERS 9 AND 10

1. What is "righteousness"?

2. Read Romans 3:21-26 and 2 Corinthians 5:21. How do we get to be declared righteous by God? What is God's part in this event? What do we do?

3. What does faith in Christ involve? Is it just a matter of believing a list of information about Him?

4. Read Romans 10:13-15. Why is fully hearing and under-standing the good news about Christ necessary for true faith?

5. In Romans 5:2, Paul writes, "through [our Lord Jesus Christ] we have gained access by faith into this grace in which we now stand." What does *standing* in grace involve for you on a typical day?

6. Read Galatians 2:20. What does it look like to live in your body by faith in the Son of God? How does this affect bodily functions like speaking, listening, eating, and commuting to work?

7. How does living by faith in the Son of God affect your response to failure at work? Your response to illness? To a tense interaction with a child or teen?

8. Bridges writes, "Any confidence in one's own religious

attainments in the issue of salvation is not only useless, but downright dangerous" (page 107). Why is this the case?

9. Read Philippians 3:4-6. What attainments have you needed (or do you still need) to throw overboard?

10. Why does Bridges think that "human morality, rather than flagrant sin, is the greatest obstacle to the gospel today" (page 110)?

11. Read Philippians 3:12-14. Why did Paul press on when he had already been justified and saved? Why didn't he just sit back and relax?

12. Bridges says, "The more a person counts as loss his own righteousness and lays hold by faith of the righteousness of Christ, the more he will be motivated to live and work for Christ" (page 113). To what degree would you say that has been your experience? Why do you suppose that's the case?

STUDY 6

CHAPTER 11 AND 12

1. Read Ephesians 2:1-3. Why do we need God to give us faith as a gift? Why can't we just decide to believe the gospel?

2. The basically decent unbelievers around us follow the ways "of the ruler of the kingdom of the air" (Ephesians 2:2)— that is, Satan. How can Paul say this? What's his evidence?

3. Does this mean we should see ourselves as better than unbelievers? Please explain.

4. Paul speaks of spiritual blindness in 2 Corinthians 4:4. Do you know anyone who is spiritually blind and unable to recognize his or her need of a Savior? If so, how does blindness affect that person's behavior?

   What are your thoughts and feelings about that person? Also, how does the blindness affect the way you treat that person? Or how you pray about him or her?

5. Read Ephesians 2:4-5. From your experience, what's it like to experience becoming spiritually alive?

6. Read 1 John 2:29; 3:1,9. What does it mean to be "born of God"?

   How does being born of God affect our thoughts, feelings, and behavior?

7. Read Romans 8:15 and Galatians 4:4-6. What's the significance

of being adopted by God? How does that affect us?

8. To what extent have you been taking advantage of the full rights of an adopted child of God? How could you do that more?

9. Read the five traits of God the Father that Bridges lists on page 132. Which of these are easy for you to see in God? Which do you struggle to believe? Why do you suppose that's the case?

10. The Scriptures in chapter 11 are full of ideas for how to pray for the unbelievers in our lives. Identify one or two people for whom you could pray. If you're meeting with a group, make a list of about ten people for whom the group can pray. Spend some time praying through Ephesians 2:1-5 and Titus 3:3-7 for each of these people. Also, take time to thank God that He has done these things for you.

11. Finally, if you're meeting with a group, pray for those members who want help to see God as a good Father.

STUDY 7

CHAPTERS 13 AND 14

1. Chapter 13 is about assurance of salvation. To what extent have you now or in the past had doubts about your salvation? (If you're meeting with a group, please understand that even if you've never struggled with doubt, many people do, and it's not something we should look down on.)

2. Read Isaiah 55:1 and Revelation 22:17. (See page 137) What does it mean to be spiritually thirsty?

   Are you or have you been spiritually thirsty? If so, what is or was that like?

3. What statements or Scriptures in chapter 13 most encourage you to be assured of your salvation?

4. Have you ever experienced the Holy Spirit's witness inside you that you are God's child? If so, what was or is that like?

5. Bridges says that a saved person's life is "characterized by an *earnest* desire and a *sincere* effort to obey God in all that He commands" (page 142). How earnestly do you want to become a person who routinely obeys God's commands? How does your desire (strong or weak) affect the way you conduct your life?

6. What should we do when awareness of our sin causes us to doubt our salvation?

7. Chapter 14 is about being like Jesus. What does it mean to be like Jesus?

8. Second Corinthians 3:18 describes a process (not a sudden event) by which we become like Jesus over time. Our part in the process involves "beholding as in a mirror the glory of the Lord." How, in practical terms, do we go about doing this?

9. What have you learned from chapter 14 about the future you can expect to experience after you die? What aspects of this are most meaningful to you?

10. What do you think about being resurrected with a body? Does it sound good to you? Surprising? Do you have any questions about the Scriptures that describe our resurrected bodies?

11. What implications does our future bodily resurrection have for our current lives with bodies?

Study 8

Chapters 15 and 16

1. According to Bridges, why shouldn't we spend our earthly lives relaxing and waiting for the good things that will happen when we're resurrected?

2. Bridges says that if we believe the gospel, we should do two things while we remain here on earth. The first is to count ourselves dead to sin. Read Romans 6:2. What's involved in counting yourself dead to sin?

3. How would you define *sanctification* in your own words?

4. William Romaine wrote, "No sin can be crucified either in heart or life, unless it be first pardoned in conscience, because there will be want of faith to receive the strength of Jesus, by whom alone it can be crucified" (page 159). What does he mean?

   How is this relevant to you?

5. To effectively keep sin from reigning in our bodies, we need to cultivate our awareness of three things: our specific sins, God's forgiveness for these sins, and the Spirit's willingness to empower us to put those sins to death. How, in practice, do we go about cultivating awareness of each of these?

6. Read John 15:1-5. What does "abiding" or "remaining" in Christ involve for a typical person on a typical day?

7. Have you experienced progressive sanctification? If so, please describe how it works in your case.

8. Horatius Bonar says, "If we would be holy, we must get to the cross, and dwell there" (page 164). How does a person dwell at the cross?

9. How do you respond to the idea that "The love of God to us, and our love to Him, work together for producing holiness" (page 164)? Is this something you've experienced? Something that sounds good but you haven't experienced?

10. The second thing Bridges says we should do with our time on earth is to participate in spreading the gospel to the ends of the earth. Why does he say spreading the gospel is so important?

11. In what ways can we participate in spreading the gospel?

12. Why do you think so few Christians devote time to praying for the spread of the gospel?

13. As you close, pray over Genesis 22:18 and Psalm 22:27-28.

NOTES

CHAPTER 1

1. M. Scott Peck, M.D., *The Road Less Traveled* (New York: Simon and Schuster, 1978), p. 15.

2. Richard Lovelace, *Dynamics of Spiritual Life* (Downers Grove, Ill.: InterVarsity, 1979), p. 101.

3. As quoted by Marsha G. Whitten, *All Is Forgiven* (Princeton, N.J.: Princeton University Press, 1993), p. 4.

4. James Buchanan, *The Doctrine of Justification* (Edinburgh: The Banner of Truth Trust, first edition 1867, reprinted May 1961), p. 236.

CHAPTER 2

1. This statement is based on information from George Smeaton in his book *The Apostles' Doctrine of the Atonement* (Edinburgh: The Banner of Truth Trust, 1991 edition), p. 15.

2. I am indebted to nineteenth-century pastor and author Henry A. Boardman for the idea of spelling out in detail what it means to obey the two great commandments. See

his own version in: Henry A. Boardman, *The "Higher Life" Doctrine of Sanctification Tried by the Word of God* (Harrisonburg, Va.: Sprinkle Publication, 1897, reprinted 1996), pp. 190-191.

CHAPTER 3

1. The statement that Jesus reaped what we have sown does not negate the application of this principle to us. It does, however, change the basis of its application. Jesus reaped the penal consequences of our disobedience. We reap the disciplinary consequences.

CHAPTER 5

1. Leon Morris, *The Atonement: Its Meaning and Significance* (Downers Grove, Ill.: InterVarsity, 1983), p. 153.

2. Some may question whether these are the words of Jesus or the words of John. In either case, however, they are words inspired by the Holy Spirit, so we can say they are the words of God.

3. George Smeaton, *The Apostles' Doctrine of the Atonement* (Edinburgh: The Banner of Truth Trust, 1991 edition), p. 311.

4. William S. Plumer, *Psalms* (Edinburgh: The Banner of Truth Trust, 1975 edition), p. 557.

5. See Romans 3:25; Hebrews 2:17; 1 John 2:2; 1 John 4:10.

6. Morris, p. 172.

7. John's record does not say Jesus cried out. However, Mark says, "With a loud cry, Jesus breathed his last," and John indicates that "It is finished" were his last words. Putting

together the two accounts, we are justified in saying, "Jesus cried out, 'It is finished.'"

8. Though believers never experience the wrath of God, we do, as occasion demands, experience the discipline of God. But the motivation behind the discipline is not God's wrath but His fatherly love. (See Hebrews 12:5-6.)

CHAPTER 7

1. George Smeaton, *The Apostles' Doctrine of the Atonement* (Edinburgh: The Banner of Truth Trust, 1991 edition), p. 248.

2. Smeaton, p. 244.

3. Smeaton, pp. 246-247.

4. Leon Morris, *The Apostolic Preaching of the Cross* (Grand Rapids, Mich.: Eerdmans, 1965), p. 59.

CHAPTER 9

1. Harold S. Kushner, *When Bad Things Happen to Good People* (New York: Avon Books, 1981), p. 6.

2. Robert H. Bainton, *Here I Stand: A Life of Martin Luther* (Nashville: Abingdon, 1950), p. 44.

3. Bainton, p. 49.

4. The third line is a late twentieth-century revision of unknown origin of Mote's original line, "I dare not trust the sweetest frame."

5. The word *now* is assumed in the NIV translation, but explicitly appears in the Greek text and in most other English translations.

6. George Smeaton, *The Apostles' Doctrine of the Atonement* (Edinburgh: The Banner of Truth Trust, 1991 edition), p. 239.

7. Benjamin Breckinridge Warfield, *The Works of Benjamin B. Warfield*, vol. VII (Grand Rapids, Mich.: Baker, 1931, reprinted 1991), p. 113.

CHAPTER 11

1. The phrase "I tell you the truth" in verses 3 and 5 is literally "truly, truly." Among the Jews the repetition of a word was intended as an emphatic statement.

2. Charles Wesley, "And Can It Be That I Should Gain?" *Worship and Service Hymnal* (Chicago: Hope Publishing Company, 1957), p. 259. This is a historic, classical hymn that appears in most standard hymnbooks. Unfortunately, some leave out this particular stanza.

CHAPTER 14

1. I used the *New American Standard Bible* (NASB) for 2 Corinthians 3:18 because of its use of *beholding* instead of *reflect* (as in the NIV). While both words accurately translate from the Greek language into English, I believe the context is more supportive of *beholding*.

CHAPTER 15

1. For the original quote, see John Brown, *Analytical Exposition of Paul the Apostle to the Romans* (Grand Rapids, Mich.: Baker, 1857, reprinted 1981), p. 93.

2. William Romaine, *The Life, Walk and Triumph of Faith* (Cambridge, England: James Clarke & Co. Ltd., 1793, 1970 edition), p. 280.

3. George Smeaton, *The Doctrine of the Holy Spirit* (Edinburgh: The Banner of Truth Trust, 1882, 1958 edition), p. 228.

4. Horatius Bonar, *God's Way of Holiness*, as quoted in *Free Grace Broadcaster*, Issue 146, October 1993, Mt. Zion Bible Church, Pensacola, Fla., p. 32.

5. The intent of this chapter is to show the relationship between the gospel and sanctification. I have addressed the practical duties of progressive sanctification in three previous books, *The Pursuit of Holiness* (1978), *The Practice of Godliness* (1983), and *The Discipline of Grace* (1994), all published by NavPress.

CHAPTER 16

1. Quoted in Michael A. G. Haykin, *One Heart and One Soul* (Durham, England: Evangelical Press, 1994), p. 164. I am indebted to Dr. Haykin for providing me the complete text of the letter in which this call to prayer was made.

2. William Carey soon joined this group of ministers and was instrumental in their forming the Baptist Missionary Society in 1792, which sent Carey to India the following year.

AUTHOR

JERRY BRIDGES is an author and Bible teacher. His most popular title, *The Pursuit of Holiness*, has sold over one million copies. He has authored several other books, including *The Discipline of Grace, The Practice of Godliness,* and *Trusting God* (all NavPress). Jerry is currently a part of the Navigator collegiate ministry group where he is involved in staff development and serves as a resource to campus ministries.

MORE LIFE-CHANGING RESOURCES BY JERRY BRIDGES.

Transforming Grace

Too many Christians misunderstand grace and try to live up to God's love. This book helps us accept and understand God's grace so we can live with the freedom of not having to measure up.

The Pursuit of Holiness

An extraordinary book that has encouraged millions of people all over the world to discover the life-giving joy of pursuing holiness. Study guide is also available.

The Practice of Godliness

All of us get caught up in doing things for God. This book is for people who want to return their focus to commitment to God rather than activities. Study guide is also available.

Trusting God

This book presents the necessary essentials of belief for the person who's seeking to trust God completely, even when things go wrong. Study guide is also available.

To get your copies, visit your local bookstore, call 1-800-366-7788, or log on to www.navpress.com. Ask for a FREE catalog of NavPress products. Offer #BPA.

NAVPRESS®

BRINGING TRUTH TO LIFE
www.navpress.com